Sangamo, a history of fifty years

Benjamin Platt Thomas, Robert Carr Lanphier

SANGAMO

*

A HISTORY OF FIFTY YEARS

JACOB BUNN
1864–1926

SANGAMO

A HISTORY OF FIFTY YEARS

FORTY YEARS OF SANGAMO

by

ROBERT C. LANPHIER

SANGAMO IN PEACE AND WAR

by

BENJAMIN P. THOMAS

PRIVATELY PRINTED

CHICAGO · 1949

Preface

LIKE most other successful American business enterprises, the Sangamo Electric Company had humble beginnings, and through the perseverance and judgment of management, mutual loyalty and understanding on the part of employer and workers, the development of technical knowledge and the courage to venture, it progressed to an established position in its field. Its story is one of long-term success, not unmixed with vicissitudes.

The story is presented here in two parts by two different authors. Part One, "Forty Years of Sangamo," was written by Robert C. Lanphier, who was co-founder of the company with Jacob Bunn and succeeded him as president. Mr. Lanphier's story is an intimate, personal narrative covering the period from 1896 to 1936. It is reproduced exactly as it was originally written and published in the latter year, and this should be remembered in reading it. For example, when Mr. Lanphier states that the Ashida Engineering Company is still Sangamo's agent in Japan, the reader must bear in mind that this was written thirteen years ago. Other statements in the

v

first part of the book are valid only as of the date when Mr. Lanphier wrote.

Part Two, "Sangamo in Peace and War," covers the period from 1936 to 1949, and is written by Benjamin P. Thomas, a long-time resident of Springfield and a distinguished historian and author. Since Mr. Thomas has no connection with the company, his narrative is less personal than Mr. Lanphier's, but he has had free access to company records and has also profited from numerous conversations with those most intimately acquainted with company affairs.

Sangamo hopes this little book—a memento of its Fiftieth Anniversary—will be of interest to those associated with the company and to its other friends.

PART ONE

FORTY YEARS OF SANGAMO
BY
ROBERT C. LANPHIER

ROBERT CARR LANPHIER

1878–1939

I

FORTY YEARS OF
SANGAMO

SANGAMO happened this way:—In 1892 the Illinois Watch Company was sued by Waltham Watch Company on the pendant set of a watch, and Tom Sheridan, as Master Mechanic of the Illinois Co., acted as principal expert for the company during this litigation.

As a result, Mr. Sheridan decided to leave and study patent law, and soon became one of the best known patent lawyers in Chicago. There, in 1895, he had as a client a Mr. Ludwig Gutmann, a German electrical engineer whose early training had been with some of the great pioneers in the electrical art, Dr. von Siemens in Berlin, Gaulard and Gibbs in France, and Blathy of Buda-Pesth. Mr. Gutmann came to the United States in 1887 and was associated with the Westinghouse Company in various engineering capacities, principally in the development of street railway motors, until early in 1895, when he went to Chicago, and shortly thereafter, to Peoria, where he became superintendent of the Royal Electric Company, manufacturers of transformers.

Prior to leaving Westinghouse, and harking back to his association with Blathy, one of the first persons to conceive of the induction watthour meter, Mr. Gutmann had also conceived the idea of such a meter, embodying several novel ideas in the, then, very primitive meter art.

It was in connection with patent applications covering these ideas that Mr. Gutmann went to Mr. Sheridan, and when he told the latter that he wanted to find a manufacturer to make his meter, Sheridan, through his former association with Illinois Watch Company, immediately thought of them, as an electric meter required a recording train, which he felt the Watch Company's equipment was suitable to produce. Furthermore, at that time, the watch business was just beginning to recover from the depression of 1893-4, so the Illinois Company had much vacant space and idle machinery, which Mr. Sheridan thought might well be utilized in the manufacture of Gutmann's meter.

Mr Bunn's first meeting with Mr. Gutmann. SO Sheridan told Mr. Jacob Bunn, Jr , then Vice President of the Watch Company, about Gutmann, early in 1896, and after a meeting with Gutmann, Mr. Bunn told his father, Mr. Jacob Bunn, Sr , about this invention, and suggested that the Illinois Watch Company consider making electric meters. However, the idea did not appeal to Mr. Bunn, Sr., so Mr. Jacob Bunn, Jr., decided to "back" Gutmann on his own account, sufficiently, at least, to find out whether there was anything to his ideas.

Mr. Bunn therefore arranged with the Watch Company to make the mechanical parts for the models Mr Gutmann wished to build, while Mr. Gutmann himself wound the coils, and assembled and tested the two models, at Peoria.

These were completed in the summer or early fall of 1896, and, as Mr. Gutmann did not have adequate testing facilities at Peoria, he sent these models to his friend, Prof. R. B Owen, Professor of Electrical Engineering at the University of Nebraska, for complete tests and for his opinion as to the commercial possibilities of such a meter.

At that time meters were not in extensive use, especially on alternating current circuits, and, outside of the Thomson commutator meter, which was then used on A.C. as well as D.C., all alternating current meters made in the United States up to 1895 were amperehour meters.

That year the Diamond Meter Co. brought out an induction watthour meter, not correct on inductive loads, but it was not until 1896 that the first true induction watthour meter was brought out by Westinghouse, embodying the Shallenberger invention of compensation to make the meter correct on inductive load.

Thus, when Prof. Owen tested Mr. Gutmann's models, there was practically no standard of good performance in induction meters to compare with, so his report simply stated that there were possibilities in the meter, when further developed and refined.

As Mr. Gutmann had neither the time nor the facilities to work out the necessary improvements, and as there was no one of electrical training associated with the Illinois Watch Co , Mr. Bunn decided to let the matter rest, for, as he told me the next year, he had spent "a couple of hundred dollars" on these models and experiments, and did not feel like throwing away more money on Mr. Gutmann's invention unless he could see some definite plan under which to develop the idea.

So the models were put away in a box in the drafting room at the Watch Company, and there they stayed through the Spring and early Summer of 1897, and there the matter might have ended except for one of those chances which often occur in this life.

Mr. Bunn first tells me of his meter venture — July 4, 1897. THE writer had graduated from Yale, in electrical engineering, in June, 1897, and came home to Springfield for a short vacation before going to Schenectady, to enter the student course of the General Electric Company, then just starting, having no thought of any electrical occupation in Springfield.

The evening of July fourth he was at a dinner where he saw Mr. Jacob Bunn, Jr., who asked about his electrical studies, and what he intended to do, then remarked, "Oh, by the way, I got interested last year, through Tom Sheridan, in some kind of electric meter invention of a man named Gutmann, who lives over in Peoria, and had a couple of models made, which are in a box out at the factory. I don't know anything about these electrical devices, so maybe, if you've learned anything at Yale, you could tell me whether there's anything to this meter." With the rashness of youth, I said I should like to see the models and Prof. Owen's report, so Mr. Bunn, with a smile, asked me to come out to the Watch Factory the next day, which I did, and we dug the box out, to find a jumbled mass of castings, coils, brass cylinders, and odds and ends.

Even with my very slight acquaintance with watt-hour meters, for little was then taught about them to electrical students, I recognized the purpose of some of the parts, and tried my best to make Mr. Bunn feel I knew "what it was all about." He very kindly suggested that I think some more about the meter during my absence on a short trip, and that he would ask Mr. Gutmann to come over to Springfield and talk to us early in August.

In the meantime, I wrote to my dear friend and teacher at Yale, Prof. Henry Bumstead, later Yale's greatest physicist, asking him to tell me where I could "read-up" on meters, and he gave me such references as he could, which were few and far between in those days.

SO, primed as best I could, I met Mr. Gutmann early in August at Mr Bunn's office, and never before nor since have I gone through such a catechism, to test my meager electrical knowledge. However, the upshot was that Mr. Gutmann told Mr.

Mr. Gutmann "cross-questions" me —August 1897

Bunn he thought "that boy" could do some experimenting with his models, "if watched carefully" as to mistakes, and Mr. Bunn then talked to me about temporarily dropping my plan of going to Schenectady, and of spending "a couple of months" trying to find out whether it would be worth while to go on with Mr. Gutmann's invention

This appealed to me, so after completing some other work I was doing for the Weather Bureau, I went out to the Watch Factory on September 13, 1897, was given a small space in which to work, and introduced to Otis White, then one of the principal tool makers in the Watch Factory machine shop, and with whom Mr. Bunn had arranged to do the fine mechanical work that I might require in the course of my experiments.

At that time the watch factory was lighted by gas made in their own plant, and had no electricity, power for the machinery being obtained from one large Corliss engine, so that I had to seek elsewhere for a place to do any experimenting. Mr. Bunn soon arranged with the old Springfield Electric Light Company, then having a power station at Seventh and Adams Sts., for me to have the use of their arc light testing rack, provided with a bank of lamps for load. That still left the question of instruments, but, after some digging around at the electric light plant, I found an old ammeter, considerably used up, which we succeeded in repairing somewhat, and with this elaborate equipment all my tests for the next few months were carried out.

As my experiments required frequent mechanical changes at the watch factory, I made a box in which to carry the rather large and heavy meter model, which I lugged back and forth on a bicycle, sometimes four or five times a day, good exercise, if not engineering experience.

M R. GUTMANN insisted, from the start, that I *Reports* should write him in detail every evening, of *required by* my experiments and results for the day, to which he *Mr. Gutmann* replied at length two or three times a week, and *on experimental* came over to Springfield, first, at intervals of a few *work.* weeks, but later, every two or three months. This report procedure was kept up for over a year, and as my letters were all in long hand, with many diagrams, they filled three big copy books, which, unfortunately, were accidentally burned up when cleaning an accumulation out of the Watch Company office a few years later.

By the latter part of November, after many, many, changes had been made in the model as I found it, especially in the adoption of spiral instead of vertical slots in the cylinder (in the belief that infringement of the Tesla patents would thus be avoided), Mr. Gutmann and I agreed that the meter was sufficiently improved to justify recommending to Mr. Bunn that a final design be made, and a small lot of meters made to such design, before considering definite plans for commercial manufacture.

So I prepared a report, which is still in our "archives," detailing my experiments, which was given to Mr. Bunn late in November, '97, and at his request, I then made in December, a perspective color drawing of the proposed meter, to show him about "what it was going to look like," which old drawing greatly faded, was resurrected in our drafting room about twenty five years later, and now hangs in my office.

After discussing the situation with Mr. Gutmann, Mr. Bunn decided to see the matter through further, at least to the extent of building some new models, so from December, '97, to March '98, Otis White and I worked on these in the Watch Company machine shop, Otis doing all the fine work, while I did the more elementary machine work, wound the coils, and assembled the models, in the meantime gaining invaluable help from Otis in the knowledge of jigs, dies and other tools.

Experimental tests at University of Illinois — Spring of 1898 WHEN the models were completed, we had no facilities in Springfield with which to make the tests on them that Mr. Gutmann wanted, so Mr. John W. Bunn, then, as for many years, Treasurer of the University of Illinois, arranged for me to use the facilities of the old electrical engineering laboratory there.

I went to Urbana in April, remaining several weeks to carry out the necessary tests and experiments, and have never forgotten the courtesies and helpful advice extended to me then by Prof. Carman, Professor of Physics.

On my return home, I prepared a report to Mr. Bunn and Mr. Gutmann, and the results indicated were such that they decided to go ahead with the manufacture of meters, but before doing so, Mr. Gutmann wanted to submit one of the models to friends in the Western Electric Company, which was therefore done in May, '98. We waited weeks for their report, and when finally received in July, were a bit discouraged by their caution regarding the danger of infringing certain patents.

However, after Mr. Gutmann had discussed the matter with his patent attorney, he told Mr. Bunn he felt there was little danger, and so far as these patents were concerned, this proved true, as they were never invoked against us.

SO, in September, 1898, Mr. Bunn decided to prepare for manufacture of Mr. Gutmann's meter, and arranged with the Watch Company for use of a few machinists, in addition to Otis White, who now began to devote all his time to the meter work.

Mr. Bunn's decision to manufacture meters — September, 1898

During the next three months, most of the tools were made, some machines bought, the old main spring building of the Watch Factory (the small building still standing at the west end of our No. 1 Building) was rented in November, and I spent that month and December fixing it up to manufacture and test meters, while Otis looked after the tools and machinery.

Our first contact with Electric Appliance Company — October, 1898

ONE day in October, while Otis and I were working in the Watch Factory machine shop, a man came in asking for "the fellow who is working on an electric meter," and when he found us, introduced himself as Levi Millard, salesman for the Electric Appliance Company, of Chicago, and said they had heard a meter was being developed in Springfield, and that they wanted the sales agency for it, if it was good. Of course I assured him it was, then took him up to Mr. Bunn, and thus began a close association that lasted as long as the Electric Appliance Company continued in business, nearly thirty years.

Early in December, Mr. Bunn and Mr. Gutmann decided to organize a small company to manufacture meters, Mr. Bunn supplying the necessary money, and Mr. Gutmann putting in his patents and pending applications. At the same time, we took on our first employe, Jim Edwards, still with us, I am glad to say, as our Senior Foreman.

How the name SANGAMO was adopted.

THERE was considerable discussion about a name for the little company, Mr. Gutmann suggesting some rather imposing ones, but Mr. Bunn finally decided on "Sangamo," because of its local interest, and the fact that it would be distinctive, should the infant company survive and grow. We have been asked many times about the origin of this name, which, in incorrect form, as "Sangamon," had been applied to our county and river. Legends differ, but the most reliable one indicates that

"Sangamo" was the name of the chief of the Illini tribe of Indians in our part of Illinois, when the first whites came there, about 1815. Years later, during the World War, a story started in New Zealand by one of our English competitors, that "Sangamo" was a Japanese name, and so great was the prejudice there against Japanese goods that we had to make a sworn statement as to the origin of our name.

WELL, with the important question of a name settled, the little Sangamo Electric Company was organized on January 11, 1899, under the laws of Illinois, with a capital of $10,000, the incorporators being Mr. Jacob Bunn, his brother Mr. Henry Bunn, and Mr. Ludwig Gutmann. Mr. Henry Bunn was elected President, Mr. Gutmann Vice President, and Mr. Jacob Bunn Secretary and Treasurer. *Incorporation of Sangamo Electric Company — January, 1899.*

That same week Mr. W. W. Low, President of the Electric Appliance Company, came down with Mr. Millard to meet Mr. Bunn, and to sign a sales contract between his company and Sangamo, and thus began a devoted friendship between Mr. Bunn and Mr. Low which lasted until Mr. Bunn's death.

By the end of January we had the little meter factory,—known then, and for many years, in the Watch Factory, as the "meter department,"— equipped and going, and had employed several more people, including one girl, to wind coils, and what a terrible job she made of it!

*First
shipment of
Gutmann
meters,
March, 1899,
and the
troubles
therewith.*

AFTER many difficulties, we completed a few meters late in March, and triumphantly shipped our first order,—from Electric Appliance Company, to the City of Logansport, Indiana, municipal electric light plant.

About two weeks later, as I was trying to test a few more meters, Mr. Bunn walked in with a yellow carbon copy of a letter from Electric Appliance Company, containing "bad news" about those Logansport meters, and I've disliked yellow paper ever since. Every one of the six meters had developed a different kind of trouble, so I had visions of an early end of the budding little Sangamo, but Mr. Bunn said we had to find out what was wrong, and I went to Logansport, my first of many "trouble-shooting" trips.

The meter man at the plant greeted me with the remark that "thems the rottenest meters I ever seen," and he was right, for on going with him to the places where five of them were installed, I found two that wouldn't run on light load, one stopped entirely, and one that hummed so loud we could hear it out in the street,—no wonder the wife of the owner told us that "my old man couldn't sleep last night account of that thing, and you'd better fix it, for he's awful sore."

So I asked them to return all the meters, and after receiving them, Mr. Gutmann came over from Peoria, and we spent some time trying to correct our troubles, the worst of which was that the meter ran on no load with the cover off. I knew this before we shipped the meters, but, in my ignorance of other meters, supposed it was to be expected, but now had to find out the cause of this serious defect. It was simple (it didn't seem so then)—we had a coil on only one leg of our U shaped shunt magnet, causing a great unbalance in field at the two pole tips adjacent to the cylinder, so when the meter was correctly adjusted before the cover was put on, the tinned steel cover shunted some of the flux at the strong side, and the meter ran backward on no load. I had therefore tested all the meters with cover on, and now found that the slightest change in position of a cover caused a change in light load accuracy.

SO we tried covers of brass and zinc, and they were all right, but expensive, then we suddenly realized that a coil on the other leg would correct the trouble. So, after a month's delay, we again started "production," and by the end of '99 had made the huge total of 540 meters. Once during the summer the Electric Appliance Co. sent us one order for fifty 10 ampere, 50 volt, 133 cycle meters, which was so huge we required nearly a month to fill it

Correction of first troubles and resumption of shipments

By the end of the year, we needed more space, so rented a small room in the next building south for painting, and the old rag shed in the back yard for a testing room, which required the sending back and forth of all meters, a boy carrying one on a hook, in each hand. That was the first job of Al Gillespie, who came with us in January, 1900, just after we moved into the new "laboratory."

I forgot to say that we now had electricity from a small 125 cycle generator in the engine room, which I had installed the previous winter, and at the same time had wired the timing and finishing rooms of the Watch Factory for electric lights, a great improvement over the old open gas lights. During 1900, the entire plant was wired, and we had our first 60 cycle service from the down town plant. A few years later, the old belt drive for power was abandoned, and motors installed throughout the Watch and Meter factories.

Sangamo's first attendance at an electrical convention, Milwaukee — January, 1900 First meeting with Tom Duncan.

IN January, 1900, we attended our first convention, the Northwestern Electrical Association, at Milwaukee, where we had a small exhibit with the Electric Appliance Company, and where I first met Tom Duncan, then, as to the end of his life, one of the best and best-known meter engineers in the country. I have never forgotten his kind attitude to me, a young and *very* green newcomer in the meter business. Thus began an intimate friendship which continued until Mr. Duncan's death in 1929.

At this time there were besides our Gutmann meter, five induction meters on the United States market: The Westinghouse round pattern "A," which had succeeded the original rectangular bulky meter of 1896; the first General Electric induction meter, as G. E. had opposed induction meters until 1898 with the Thomson commutator meter; the Ft. Wayne (Duncan) meter, succeeding their Slattery amperehour A.C. meter brought out about 1893;

the Schieffer, improved over the original of 1895; and the Stanley, famous for the magnetic flotation of its moving system, the most advanced in design of all.

The little Sangamo company thus faced severe competition, plus the probability of patent litigation, which was actually started against us in the spring of 1901 by Westinghouse, under the famous Tesla patents covering the operation of an induction motor on single phase current.

In the meantime, Sangamo made considerable headway in 1900 with the cylinder type Gutmann meter, which, that spring, was shortened in dimension from the wall, and otherwise improved, though still not compensated for inductive load Production that year therefore reached the large total of about 2000 meters, so the little company managed to remain in existence, but that was about all.

IT was at this time, probably the early spring of 1901 that the oval Sangamo emblem came into existence. We had been trying to work the name into some kind of trade-mark, and one day I sketched an oval outline, with Sangamo in conventional straight letters. When I showed it to Mr. Bunn, he said it needed "some style," and suggested I show it to Granville Kindred, then head engraver at the Watch Factory, and a skilled designer. "Granny" looked at it a moment, then said, "why don't you give the letters a wiggle, to make them look like lightning had hit them, since you're an electric con-

How the oval SANGAMO trade-mark came about.

cern?" Then, with a few strokes of his skilful pencil, he made a beautiful design, which we have used ever since, in every country on earth, in fact, the oval Sangamo was long since registered as a trademark in nearly thirty countries.

By the early part of 1901, it was evident that we would have to make a radical change to further increase our sales, which was emphasized on a trip I made to Memphis, then one of our best customers, in April. The General Manager there, Mr. Proutt, was a very able, clear thinking, and fair-minded engineer, and during my visit gave me most valuable suggestions, which, on return home, I discussed with Mr. Gutmann, and we then decided to experiment with a disk armature, instead of the cylinder, the general principle of operation being otherwise the same as in our first meter.

Development of the disk type Gutmann meter — Summer of 1901. THE disk type Gutmann meter was therefore developed during the next three months, compensation for inductive load being added, and during the late summer tools were made, so that the first meter was assembled in September, and I took it to Memphis, for Mr. Proutt's approval, which he gave.

During my absence for a month, from the middle of October, for the important purpose of a wedding trip, made possible by Mr. Bunn's consideration and kindness, a few meters were produced, the first of which was sent to me at Montreal, where I "demonstrated" it to our original Canadian agent, Mr.

John Forman, who had started selling Gutmann meters the previous spring, our first export business. He and his men were as enthusiastic about the new meter as I was, but on my return home in November, I found plenty of trouble with the few meters that had been finished, principally in absence of torque, and consequent erratic performance. The situation was particularly bad because the Electric Appliance Company had gotten a large order— some 600 meters—from the City of Tacoma, and the customer was more than irate because of delayed shipment.

So Mr. Gutmann came over, and after a week of working together, we added some iron in the series coils, and thus got up to the large (!) torque of 15 millimeter-grams, which wasn't bad for those days. We soon shipped the Tacoma meters, but I've never forgotten the prepaid express bill we had to pay to get them there promptly.

The new meter, backed by the enthusiasm of the Electric Appliance Company, and especially that of I. A. Bennett, their General Sales Manager, "took hold" rapidly, and by the early spring of 1902 we were making over forty meters a day, a good volume considering the small meter business of that day, and the strong competition we faced. Our position was further strengthened by the fact that we now had the first meter with a separately accessible bottom terminal box, a cover with screws sealed at the back, and that we were the first to offer glass covers without extra charge.

DURING these months since the spring of 1901, we had retained as our patent counsel Mr. Charles A. Brown, of the Chicago firm of Barton and Brown, with whom Mr. Gutmann had had previous satisfactory experience. Mr. Brown, as a very young man, had been General Manager of the Western Electric Company, then, aided by Mr. Enos Barton, the President of that company, he left to study patent law, and soon after he completed this work, became the partner of Mr. George Barton, brother of Mr. Enos Barton. Mr. Brown was (and is today) a man of great ability, and assumed our defence, in the several suits that had been filed against us, with vigor and enthusiasm. He chose as our principal expert Prof Dugald C Jackson, then head of the department of Electrical Engineering at the University of Wisconsin, later to become famous as head of the electrical department of Massachusetts Institute of Technology, and as President of the A. I. E. E.

None of the early patent suits were brought directly against us as a manufacturer, but against agents and users in scattered places, one of the principal purposes in patent litigation in those days being to thus cause added expense of defence to small, struggling competitors like ourselves

The principal suits, therefore, in which we were concerned in 1901 to 1903, were one against the H. C. Roberts Supply Company of Philadelphia, our Eastern agent at that time, and the other against the Mutual Life Insurance Company of

N. Y., who used our meters in their building in Elmira, N. Y.

Mr Brown soon obtained an agreement with the Westinghouse attorneys, Kerr, Page and Cooper of New York, that testimony should first be taken in the Roberts case, and this was started in the late fall of 1901, continuing, at Chicago and New York, at various times throughout 1902, during which I received my "baptism" in patent matters, expensive, but valuable in later years.

In addition to Prof. Jackson as principal expert, we engaged a number of other very prominent engineers, who testified for us, including Prof. William B. Anthony, of New York, one of the founders and Past President of A. I. E. E., Prof. Kennelly of Harvard, Mr. William H. Barstow, and others.

Our defenses were, first, that Tesla was fully anticipated in his invention by the great Prof. Ferraris, of Turin, second, that our mode of operation, on account of the spiral slots in our disk, and the arrangement of the fields, was not the same as Tesla had disclosed, and thirdly, even if one and two were rejected,—that Tesla was anticipated by several others in this art.

In preparing the defense of our case, I spent much time with Prof. Jackson at Madison and Springfield during the Spring and Summer of 1902, getting many valuable ideas from him. We made many experiments in his laboratory at Madison, and also at Springfield, in the attempt to sustain our position.

IN the meantime, we were seeking an outlet for our meters in New York and New England, and in May, 1902—through Mr. Low,—Mr. Bunn and I met Mr. E. W. Rockafellow, Apparatus Sales Manager of the Western Electric Company at New York, who recommended to his superiors, Mr. Thayer and Mr. Wilkins, that they sell Gutmann meters.

So the deal was made, and late in June Mr. Bunn and I went to New York, where he signed the agreement with Western, and I "talked meters" to all their Eastern District salesmen, who had been called together for that purpose.

The eventful day was concluded by a celebration party given by Mr. Bunn at the old Cafe Lafayette, which I have never forgotten.

Within a few weeks, the Western salesmen had sold Gutmann meters in a great number of towns, and we were delighted, but our happiness was short lived, as Westinghouse sued for an injunction against Western within a few weeks.

Unfortunately, our counsel, Mr. Brown, had severed his connection with Mr. George Barton, on account of some personal difference with Mr. Enos Barton, President of Western Electric, so, when we told the latter that Mr. Brown would defend, at our expense, the injunction proceedings against Western, Mr. Barton told us that Mr. Brown could not appear in any case for them, but offered to defend the suit through their own attorneys, without expense to us.

Much as Mr. Bunn appreciated this, it was obvious that we had to stick by Mr. Brown, and we so advised Mr. Barton.

So when the injunction hearing took place the end of August, Western Electric entered no answer, we were not represented, and the preliminary injunction was entered against Western, thus ending their fine effort to sell our meters after only two months.

DURING the taking of testimony in New York in April, 1902, I met Nikola Tesla for the first time, and he impressed me then as a very unusual, excitable and brilliant man. Years later, in 1918, he telephoned me one day to come to see him in New York at once on an urgent, secret matter connected with the defense of our country, so I went, and left him, after a six hour discussion, with the feeling that his thoughts and ideas were not of this earth,—certainly the idea he put up to me, for Sangamo's cooperation, sounded like a Buck Rogers' dime novel.

My first meeting with Nikola Tesla — April, 1902

DURING 1902 our business increased very satisfactorily, notwithstanding patent litigation, and the heavy expense thereof for our small company, and by the early part of 1903, we were faced with a pressing need for more space, so the Watch Company agreed to erect a building for us, our present Number One, which was started in the summer, and completed that Fall. We were just occupying it, when the crash of the decision in the Roberts' suit came down on us.

Construction of No. 1 Building — Summer, 1903

Injunction against Sangamo in Roberts' case at Philadelphia — September, 1903. THE hearing in this case took place before Judge Archbold, of Philadelphia in January 1903, and for some reason he failed to hand down a decision until late in September, in which he upheld the Tesla patents against the Roberts Company, and gave the injunction asked for by Westinghouse.

Sales arrangement with Brush Electrical Engineering Co., London — Mr. Bunn's visit to England — Summer, 1903. IN the meantime, we had started negotiations in the spring of 1903 with the Brush Electrical Engineering Company of London, to sell our meters in Great Britain, and Mr. Bunn went to England in July to close the contract with them. On his return late in September, I greeted him at New York with the bad news about the Roberts' case, and, as usual, he said, "Well, we're not licked yet."

However, it soon looked as though we might be, for, following the injunction against the Roberts Company, Mr. Brown, our counsel, told us to disregard it, as we were not the actual party defendant, so we kept on making meters through October.

Injunction against Sangamo and termination of Gutmann meter production — November 11th, 1903. THEREUPON, the Westinghouse Company asked Judge Archbold to adjudge us in contempt of court if we failed to respect the injunction, so on November 11, 1903, he granted this action, and Mr. Bunn, who was in Chicago, telephoned me to stop all operations that night, a great shock to all connected with Sangamo.

During the balance of November and all of December we retained only a few employes,—in the hope of a successful appeal from Judge Archbold's decision (which we never obtained), also of carrying on in Canada, and finally, of developing quickly the mercury motor direct current meter, on which Mr. Gutmann had started me experimenting as far back as the spring of 1902,—but on which we had not made much progress.

IN December, Federal Judge Kohlsaat, of Chicago, granted a plea made by Mr. Brown, permitting us to ship all our stock of finished Gutmann meters, nearly all of which were in the Electric Appliance Company warehouse in Chicago, to Canada, or elsewhere outside the United States, on the ground that the Tesla patents covered a "system of operation," and not merely the motor—i.e. the meter—connected in the system, so that infringement did not exist until the meter was in operation. This was a God-send to us, especially as Mr. Bunn then went to Montreal, and through our agent, Mr. Forman, sold the entire lot of meters to the Montreal Light, Heat and Power Company. Not long thereafter, when in Montreal, I met a young man about my age named Donaldson then in the meter department of the Montreal Company. Years later, when we started British Sangamo, I had the pleasing surprise of meeting him again as Captain Donaldson, Managing Director of the North Metropolitan Electric Supply Company of London, for many years since then our largest customer in England.

Shipment of finished Gutmann meters to Canada and first manufacturing at Windsor — January, 1904.

Under Judge Kohlsaat's decision, we were also free to manufacture parts for meters, and even assemble them, so long as we did not operate them on current, so, taking advantage of this, we decided to start a small assembling and testing plant in Canada, to supply our trade in Canada and England, also in Mexico, Japan and some other foreign countries, in which we had a fair business for those days.

So, at the end of December, Mr. Bunn and I went to Detroit, to find a location in Windsor, across the river. En route, we were in Chicago December 30th, and tried to get seats for the performance at the Iroquois Theatre that afternoon. Fortunately for us, there were none to be had, so we took the afternoon train to Detroit, and at Kalamazoo learned of the terrible Iroquois fire, with the loss of nearly 600 lives.

After several days search at Windsor, we found a second floor store-room, so I remained several weeks in January 1904 fitting this up, assisted by Frank Pride, who came up from Springfield, and remained in charge of our little place at Windsor,—later transferred to Walkerville,—until we found the venture so unprofitable that we discontinued it after two years, not to resume manufacturing in Canada until many years later.

Development of first mercury motor meter — 1904

DURING December, 1903, Henry Hodde (alias "Dutch") started working with me to develop the mercury meter, our only hope for business in the United States.

By this time Mr. Gutmann had ceased to have a very active connection with us, although still retaining his interest and position in the company, so the development of the mercury meter was carried on by Otis White, Dutch Hodde and myself, and as I think back to all the wild schemes we tried during the first six months of 1904, to make a meter reasonably accurate on light load, and on change in voltage, I realize how little we all knew then about mercury meters.

Fortunately, Mr. Bunn was patient and understanding, as always, even though we were losing money (that we did not have) month after month, so, encouraged by him, we tooled up the original type "C" mercury meter in the summer, and produced the first lot in August.

THESE meters were shipped in September, on order from the Electric Appliance Company, to Oneida, Illinois, a small town near Galesburg, and it was another case like Logansport, only worse, for when I received a frantic call to go over there early in October, I found the mercury had leaked out of the armature chamber of *every* single meter! During my two days' stay there, the situation was made more enjoyable by having to sleep on a cot in a livery stable.

First type C mercury meters shipped September, 1904 to Oneida, Illinois and the troubles with them

The trouble proved to be in the material used for the mercury chamber,—Electrose,—a shellac and mica compound, which we found would soften at about 125 degrees F., which had never occurred to us at all. The meters at Oneida had been piled up in the boiler room of the plant, with resultant temperature well above the softening point of the Electrose.

So we now had to find a more heat resistant material, and while Hodde experimented at Springfield, I went to the Electrose Company, at Brooklyn, and others, in the endeavor to get such material. The Electrose Company were very helpful, and by adding asbestos fibre and reducing the proportion of shellac in the mixture, they produced for us in about two months, a brown material, which proved sufficiently heat resistant. Thus, in December, 1904, we finally got started on the production of type "C" meters that seemed satisfactory, and during 1905 we shipped several thousand of these meters.

Development of mercury motor watthour meter — 1905

HOWEVER, the type "C" was neither a true watthour meter nor an amperehour meter, so Hodde and I continued experiments to the end of obtaining a watthour meter, no mercury watthour meter having been made, up to that time, in England, the birthplace of mercury meters, or elsewhere.

We obtained the desired result in the summer of 1905 by the simple expedient of adding damping magnets and a damping disk carried on the armature shaft, outside the mercury chamber, and four meters of this construction were built as models, and sent to Denver and Peoria for test in July 1905. The results reported were so satisfactory that we decided to supersede the type "C" with the new "type D," on which tooling was started at once, and the first meters produced in November.

In passing, it is interesting to note that the original model type "D" sent to Peoria was in successful use there, at the Block & Kuhl store, for over twenty years, until destroyed in a fire.

G OING back to the litigation on the induction meter, Mr. Brown endeavored during 1904 to have the injunction against us set aside, but lost on appeal, and the Westinghouse Company then demanded an accounting and damages. After hearings over several months, a decision on this matter was rendered in January 1905, and, Mr. Brown having then ceased to be our counsel, Mr. Bunn engaged Mr. Carl Meyer, one of the best known lawyers in Chicago (then and now) to go with us to New York, and negotiate a settlement with Westinghouse and General Electric, who, under their patent agreement of those days with Westinghouse, were a party to the matter.

Settlement of Tesla patent litigation with Westinghouse Company — January, 1905

Our opponents, represented by Mr. Charles Neave, a classmate at Yale of Mr. Meyer's, started off with impossible demands, a royalty of five dollars per meter on the 30,000 we had made, both cylinder and disk type, and also demanded we go out of business failing our agreement to which demands one of their attorneys said they would go after all our users, and make them remove the meters. Mr. Meyer told them emphatically that their demands were ridiculous, that "one couldn't squeeze blood out of a turnip," and that Sangamo would *not* go out of business.

We wrangled with them until lunch time, and I always felt that the appearance of Mr. George Westinghouse himself during these hours, and some conciliatory remarks he made, had a helpful effect for us. At any rate, when Mr. Bunn, Mr. Meyer and I went down to lunch in the old "Savarin" cafe, Mr. Meyer said, "We will pay them $15,000.00 or about fifty cents per meter, if you say so, but not a cent more." Mr. Bunn said we had no such sum, but that if I felt we could build a meter to get around the situation, he would find the money. So, somewhat rashly, I said we could, and we went up after lunch, Mr. Meyer made the offer, and, after some argument, Mr. Neave told our opponents to accept it. They did so, then again urged Mr. Bunn to get out of the meter business, offering him to cancel the indemnity, to buy all tools, equipment, material, etc., so as to leave the company a nice profit, and to provide positions for Mr. White and myself.

To most men this would have been a tempting "out" on a bad situation, but not Mr. Bunn, for he politely declined, and we took the next train to Chicago The next afternoon Mr. Bunn, Mr. Low, Mr. Meyer and I were at the Chicago Athletic Club, when he received a telegram from the attorneys of Westinghouse again urging him to consider a still more liberal offer. He handed it to me, and said,

"Those fellows seem mighty anxious, and now it's up to you, for you have a good offer from them, whereas if you stick with Sangamo, we may eventually have to go under, and I don't want to stand in your way. Besides, I can come out all right, and with some profit, if I take their offer." Of course I said I would stay with him, if he wanted to keep on, so Mr. Meyer and Mr. Low both urged him not to give in, we all shook hands, had a wee bit to celebrate, and Mr. Bunn wired back that he respectfully declined the offer

ON return to Springfield, the first question was about the $15,000.00 we had to pay, and, as the company had no money, and as Mr. Gutmann, the principal stockholder besides Mr. Bunn, was unable to pay an assessment on his stock, Mr. Bunn offered to buy his interest at par, which Mr. Gutmann accepted in March, 1905, and then terminated his connection with Sangamo. Mr. Bunn then furnished the money to pay Westinghouse, and we turned our thoughts entirely to mercury meters, realizing that we could not again make induction meters until after expiration of the Telsa patents. By this time, the Schieffer Company had quit, and the Stanley Company had been enjoined after suit on the Tesla patents, leaving Westinghouse and General Electric (including their Fort Wayne meter) meters alone in the induction meter field until these patents expired in December, 1910.

Payment of indemnity to Westinghouse and rearrangement of Sangamo stock holdings.

NO sooner had we settled with Westinghouse than we were sued, in April, 1905, by General Electric on our D.C mercury meter, under four or five of their patents, the principal one being a patent of Halsey's, who had made a few mercury ampere hour meters in Chicago from 1900 to 1903, and had then sold his patents to General Electric. The only claim of serious concern to us was one covering the complete amalgamation of the disk, and on this, after three years litigation, conducted for us by Mr. C. E. Pickard, of Bond, Adams, Pickard & Jackson, —we were defeated, but won on all other counts, and caused one of the G. E patents to be invalidated, because of incorrect practice in connection with its issue.

We then resorted to partial amalgamation of the disk, but after a short time, early in 1909, entered into a mutual license agreement with General Electric, permitting us to utilize their patents as well as our own, and thus began the friendly and co-operative relations we have had with them ever since.

IN the meantime, going back to 1905, we had a severe jolt that fall, just as the type "C" was being superseded by the type "D," for one day Bert Brinkerhoff, who had come with us after graduating at Cornell the previous June, came to me with a type "C" meter returned on account of mercury leaking, and called my attention to the contact ears showing amalgamation *outside* the mercury chamber. We broke the ears out, and my heart sank when I saw them both completely amalgamated, the mercury having slowly worked its way across the copper from inside, for this meant that every type "C" meter we had sent out in the ten months of their production, must inevitably develop the same trouble sooner or later, *and they did*.

The trouble was due to my having stupidly overlooked the fact that the copper ears should have been enameled, or nickel plated, to avoid this obvious danger, and it was cured at once by nickel plating, so that very few type "D" meters got out with the leaky ears.

I went over to tell Mr. Bunn that we faced the prospect of replacing or taking back all the type "C" meters we had made, expecting some strong remarks on the blunder I had made, but, characteristically, he merely said, "Well, now what do you think of that! Those things will happen, and I hope your scheme of nickel-plating will do the trick." And that's all he ever said about it, even after hundreds of meters came back.

BY this time, the Electric Appliance Company was pressing us to get up an A.C. meter that would not infringe any patents, and early in 1906, I had the temerity to build a meter, the idea of which had occurred two years before, and on which we obtained patents, the scheme being to put a condenser in series with the shunt coil of the "Type D" meter, adjusted to make a resonant circuit at the

The condenser type alternating current mercury meter— 1906.

desired frequency, and thus giving a true A.C watthour measurement at *that* frequency.

Unfortunately, frequencies were not well regulated in those days, variations of 3 or 4 percent being the usual thing, except on a few large 60 cycle systems, which frequency was then just coming into more general use, so after sending out a few hundred of these "condenser type" meters, in the spring of 1906, we soon had many complaints. I went up to Hammond, Indiana, where they then had 133 cycles, to investigate our worst complaint, and then realized that what we were making was rather a frequency meter than a watthour meter, so another hope was blasted, and nearly all these condenser meters came back.

Our sulphur impregnated condenser.

HOWEVER, we did one interesting and satisfactory job in developing this meter, a sulphur impregnated cylindrical paper condenser, of which we later sold quite a large quantity.

The transformer type alternating current mercury meter — 1906

WE now sought some other way of operating a mercury meter on alternating current, and after a short time, hit on a really correct idea, namely, what we later called our "transformer meter," in which the mercury chamber was connected across a very low potential secondary (about 1/30 volt) of a small potential transformer in the meter, and series coils, carrying the load current, were placed on the electromagnet, instead of the shunt coils of the Type "D" meter. This meter had some really remarkable characteristics, being inherently correct on inductive load, and, when built for 25 cycles, had practically the same accuracy on any frequency up to 80 or more cycles.

Years later, and long after we again made induction meters, we built some of these A C. mercury meters for use on circuits where the frequency was varied over wide limits for motor speed control, a condition for which no induction meter could be used.

We had a hard time convincing the patent office that the mode of operation of this meter was workable, and I finally spent three days in Washington with Mr. Pickard, arguing with the examiner. However, after taking the examiner to the Willard Hotel and operating a meter, he allowed our claims.

We brought out the first transformer meters, which we called the type "E," soon after the demise of the condenser meter, in June, 1906, and thought we were at last out of the woods, especially as the meter sold well, almost from the start.

IT was also about this time that we began making our own mercury chambers, having worked out a shellac-mica-asbestos mixture that gave us a harder and more heat resistant chamber than those supplied us by the Electrose Manufacturing Company, and we continued to use this material until we went over to Bakelite early in 1912, the year after Dr. Baekeland announced this material. We were thus one of the first three companies to use

Beginning of our own production of molded mercury chambers— 1906 —Bakelite, 1912.

Bakelite, and I believe no other piece has been made of Bakelite, unchanged in design, as long as our D-5 mercury chamber.

Agency arrange-
ments—1906
and 1907.

SHORTLY before this, in the early spring of 1906, we made our second agency arrangement outside of Electric Appliance Company and H. C. Roberts (excepting the short ill-fated connection with Western Electric), with the Wesco Supply Company, of St. Louis, who became very active for our meters, and did a very effective business for us throughout the Southwest during the next six years, standing by us splendidly through the troubles and disappointments of that period, as, in fact, all our agents except one, did.

That exception was Machado and Roller, who began selling our meters in the New York territory in 1905, and were very helpful until 1910, when Mr. Roller decided Sangamo's future looked dark, and assumed the agency for another meter, which, in a few years, disappeared from the market.

Early in 1906 we were very fortunate in making a sales arrangement for the Pittsburgh territory with Mr. Ludwig Hommel, which has continued ever since with mutual satisfaction, so we take very great pride in this connection

A little later, in May, 1906, Mr. Bunn had a letter from two young fellows who had just started out for themselves in Boston "on a shoestring"—Bruce Wetmore and Hanson Savage—and how they made that shoestring grow! So Mr. Bunn and I went to see them, finding Bruce in their tiny office on Oliver Street, while "Hans" was out selling.

It didn't take long to decide we wanted each other, so that evening, when "Hans" got back, the contract was signed with suitable celebration, and for nearly twenty years Wetmore-Savage did a remarkable business for us in the New England territory. Later, following the death of Hans Savage in 1923, Bruce Wetmore, to our great regret, decided to sell the business. We have never had finer relations with any one than with these two men. However, we were fortunate in having had with them, as our expert, since 1911, Staff King, who came with us January first, 1925, to handle the New England territory, which he has done so successfully ever since.

And in the spring of 1907 we made one of the most important sales connections in our history, when I went to Philadelphia and met George Rumsey. He and his brother had established the Rumsey Electric Company there some ten years before, and had already gained a fine reputation for energetic and honest sales work, so we were glad to enlist them as our agents for the Philadelphia territory, and on south to the Carolinas. This connection, I am happy to say, continues most satisfactorily to this day.

Thus, during 1906 and 1907, we formed many of our most valuable and lasting agency connections.

RETURNING now to our factory history, I have to tell of one of the most unexpected and interesting experiences we ever had, which occurred in the spring of 1906. One day I had a telegram from Mr. William Stanley, sent from the train at Albany, asking me to meet him the next day at a hotel in Chicago. Of course, his name, one of the greatest in the electrical history of this country, was well-known to me both from his early connection as the first electrical engineer of the Westinghouse Company, as founder, in 1890, of the Stanley Electric Company, and later, as inventor of the Stanley meter, but I had never met him. So I went, and found him to be one of the most interesting and delightful men I had ever met, full of ideas, the principal one at the moment being the plan he put before me, of saving what was left of his company, which, like ourselves, had been enjoined under the Tesla patents, by combining it with Sangamo. With him was that truly remarkable man, Guiseppe Faccioli, who had invented a reciprocating type meter for A.C. and D.C , and who had also worked out an induction type meter of Mr. Stanley's own invention, which he felt would escape the Tesla patents, and thus, with our mercury meters, give the nucleus of a meter business that could maintain itself.

This meter of Mr Stanley's had two disks, one responding to a shaded pole driving field carrying a flux equal to (a+b), "a" being current, and "b" voltage, the other disk operating in an (a−b) field, so that the resultant effect, at the spindle, was equal to "4 a b," in other words, watthours.

That night, until a very late hour, I sat spellbound listening to those two brilliant men, as they planned how we were going to work together, but after Mr. Stanley had spent a week in Springfield, then made a second visit a few weeks later, the plan did not seem practicable to Mr. Bunn, Mr. Pickard (our patent attorney) and to me, and we so advised Mr. Stanley. Soon afterward he became a consultant of the General Electric Company, so continuing to the end of his life, while Faccioli went with them at Pittsfield, and, notwithstanding great physical suffering, became one of the greatest—probably *the* greatest—transformer engineer in the world.

SHORTLY after this interesting episode, we ran into a new and serious trouble with our mercury meters, as all of our product was then, consisting in loss of buoyancy of the moving system, and consequent stopping, even on heavy load. This came about through my having failed to realize that the necessary flotation of the armature could be obtained by the use of a small cylinder of wood, or composition, attached to the armature disk, instead of which Otis White had gone to much trouble to develop a hollow copper dome, riveted over a raised groove in the disk. This worked fine for a time, but eventually, in many meters, the mercury amalgamated its way through this joint, the float chamber filled with mercury, and the moving sys-

More mercury meter trouble, —sinking armatures. 1907 —My trip to Texas— the "yellow dog" story.

tem became a "sinker," as we called these after the trouble developed.

Again, as in the case of leaking contact ears a year before, it required only the simple change to a wood float (later replaced by bakelite, as still used) to eliminate the trouble, but, again, we had hundreds of meters out in which armatures eventually had to be replaced.

The worst of this trouble, for some reason, occurred in the type "E" alternating current meters, and to a great extent in Texas, probably due to average higher temperatures there which hastened the leakage into the floats. By the spring of 1907, the situation there was so serious that both Electric Appliance Company at Dallas, and Wesco, at Ft. Worth, insisted I come down to try to pacify some of their customers, so I went, and never have I forgotten that harrowing trip! First I went down to Del Rio, on the Rio Grande River, to repair some sixty meters that had gone bad, and what with terrific heat, Mexican food, and poor facilities for testing, I was glad to leave after nearly a week's work.

Then I went to Dallas, and Bill Upham, branch manager there for Electric Appliance Company, told me he had several customers for me to see, but that the most irate was a big fellow named Brown at Ennis, not far from Dallas, and that he didn't know what Brown might do if I went there. So, of course, we went, and Bill introduced me, not as a Sangamo factory man, but as "a young fellow who is with us

at Chicago." Bill had warned me, above all, not to
refuse a drink if Brown offered it, which he promptly
did, and after one or two more, got around to "those
damned Sangamo meters" and what he said was
finally topped off by the remark, "if I had a poor
yaller dog named Sangamo, I'd drown the damn'
thing!" Well, then I had to summon up courage to
tell him I was responsible for those meters, and that
we now had them fixed up all right. For a minute
I thought he was going to throw me out, then he
grabbed the bottle and said, "Boy, have another,
you're all right!" We parted sworn friends, and Mr.
Brown stuck with us thereafter.

EARLY in 1907, we got our first business outside
of meters, when the Wheeler and Schebler
Carburetor Company of Indianapolis asked us to
make the permanent magnets for a magneto they
were just bringing out, and during the next two
years this developed into a good-sized and profitable
business. To meet this demand, we required more
space than we then had in one of the Watch Company sheds, just south of our No. 1 building, where
we started making our own magnets in 1906, so the
Watch Company built for us, in 1907, our present
forge shop, where, for many years, we used oil fur-
naces for hardening as well as forming.

Permanent magnets for Schebler Carburetor Co.—1907

LATE in that year, we began to think of making
a high tension magneto ourselves, to compete
with Bosch and others then on the market, and dur-

Our experiments with magnetos—1908.

ing 1908 Bert Brinkerhoff, Dutch Hodde, Otis White and I made a number of experimental models of a high tension magneto without the customary "make-and-break," but by the middle of 1909 it seemed best not to continue this effort, and it was dropped.

Type F for A.C. and type D-5 for D C mercury meters—1909.

DURING the early part of 1908, we greatly improved the construction of our mercury meter, and in 1909, brought out the type "F" for A.C., shortly followed by the D-5 for D.C., practically the same, in all respects, as our present D.C. meter, and we then thought we would never go back to an induction meter.

The birth of the amperehour meter — Ernest Lunn— 1908.

ABOUT this time, at the N. E. L. A. Convention in Chicago, in May, 1908, I had the good fortune to meet Mr. Ernest Lunn, then Superintendent of Storage Batteries of the Commonwealth Edison Company, through our good friend of so many years, Mr. O. J. Bushnell, Superintendent of the Meter Department of that company.

He had been trying to get, or develop, an amperehour meter for use with their great standby batteries, and, when Mr. Bushnell told him we made mercury motor meters, Lunn said he would like to see what we could do for him. So we quickly produced a model by substituting a powerful permanent magnet for the shunt field of our watthour meter, and submitted this to him in August.

He was so pleased with it that he asked for several

more to try out on electric trucks of the Edison Company, as well as for use with several of their stand-by batteries. We delivered the meters in October, and thus the amperehour meter business was born, so valuable to us ever since.

Mr. Lunn then suggested to us that the amperehour meter should have a valuable application with batteries on electric lighted railway cars, and in December we submitted meters to the Pennsylvania, Wabash, and several other roads, with the result that they were immediately applied on a number of cars with straight storage systems, that is, without charging equipment on the car, such batteries being charged between trips at terminal points. However, the majority of railroad cars then, and practically all a few years later, had full automatic equipment, the battery being charged, above a certain train speed, from a generator driven from the car axle, and therefore discharging at one moment, and charging at another. This necessitated an amperehour meter arranged to run slower on charge than on discharge, in order to give the battery the necessary overcharge, but it was not until 1912 that we solved this problem, as related later.

In the meantime, for meters used on electric vehicles, or wherever the cycles of charge and discharge were entirely separated, the necessary difference in speed was obtained by the "differential shunt," developed early in 1909, and successfully used for several years. Again, as with the "transformer type" A.C. mercury meter, we had a struggle with the patent office, as our claims on the "differential shunt" were, at first, rejected on the ground that the arrangement of divided circuits described in our application constituted an ordinary Wheatstone bridge arrangement, and furthermore, would not accomplish the result we claimed. Again I went to Washington, this time with Mr. John L. Jackson, who, I am happy to say, still handles our patent matters. He had taken over our patent work after the death of his partner, Mr. Pickard in 1909.

Mr. Jackson and I found the examiner reasonable, but very dubious, but as before, we set up a differential shunt meter with a battery, proved it would do what we claimed, and soon got our patent.

*Sales problems
—1909–10 —
I. A. Bennett's
connection
with us*

SO, with the amperehour meter safely launched, I turn back to our principal product, watthour meters. The market for D.C. meters, never large as compared with A.C. meters, steadily decreased. By 1909 we had to rely principally on our Type "F," A.C. mercury meter, and we found it a big task to sell it against General Electric and Westinghouse induction meters. These meters were the only ones on the U. S. market from 1905 to 1911, as all other manufacturers were stopped by litigation until the Tesla patents expired in December, 1910.

Feeling the need for the best sales direction, in this situation, we turned to our old friend, I. A. Bennett, formerly Sales Manager of E. A. Company and now in business for himself in Chicago, and during the latter part of 1909 and through the summer of 1910, he spent half his time in Springfield, putting much able and ingenious effort on the task of selling our mercury meters, but his dual responsibilities were too great a strain, and he discontinued his work for us about the time that we realized, in the summer of 1910, that we must develop a new induction meter, and get ready to put it on the market after the expiration of the Tesla patents. So we started on this development at the same time the Watch Company was erecting for us our present No. 3 building, the first of many designed for us by Mr. George Helmle, which was completed in the late fall of 1910.

ABOUT this time I met Mr. Herbert W. Young, who had been a very successful salesman for the Westinghouse Company in New England, especially on meters, and who had recently started his own company, Delta-Star Electric of Chicago, to manufacture high tension switch-gear. I proposed to him that he devote part of his time to our sales, as Delta Star was then far from the great company it became later, so Young had time to give our affairs, and decided to accept our proposition.

H. W. Young comes with us in charge of sales—1911.

WE then hastened experimental work on what became the original type "H" meter, in which I was assisted by Hodde, most of our work being done at night in the old testing room at the east end of the second floor of No. 1 building, as we had no engineering department, and, in fact, few experi-

Development of the type H meter—Fall of 1910.—The Hartford order. Production of first meters— January, 1911

mental facilities up to this time. In November, 1910, we had just completed and tested a rather crude model, when Herb Young had the bright idea of going to Hartford, Conn., where he had close friends through his old connection in New England, and trying to get a small trial order for the new-born "H" meter. So we went, our sole "evidence" being a couple of blueprints, and some data I had taken on the one model—I didn't dare to show our "prospect" the model itself! Never shall I forget that visit, which, as it turned out, meant so much to Sangamo, for, after meeting Fred Prince, then Meter Superintendent of the Hartford Electric Light Company, we all went together to see Mr. Matthew Dunham, President of the Company, and one of the most remarkable figures the electrical industry has ever had. He was then 82 years old, almost totally blind, a majestic and kindly man with a long white beard, a true patriarch in appearance and character, and, notwithstanding his advanced years, one of the most progressive and far-seeing men in the electric light and power business. He was the first in this country to use long distance transmission commercially, the first to use stand-by storage batteries, the first to offer free lamp renewals, and first in numerous other steps important to the company and its customers.

As soon as Fred Prince told him Herb Young was there, he was friendly and interested, having developed a great liking for Herb when the latter was selling in New England. Herb introduced me with the remark that I had gone to Yale, of which Mr. Dunham was one of the most distinguished alumni (and to which he gave the Dunham Laboratory of Electrical Engineering about this time), so the old gentleman remarked that with *that* recommendation and Herb's and Fred Prince's statement to him that we would have a good meter, he thought they ought to try some. Herb and I fairly jumped with joy, expecting a trial order for perhaps twenty four meters, when Mr. Dunham took us completely off our feet by saying, "Now, boys, I'm taking you at your word, and believe you will give us good meters, and I like to encourage good competition, so I guess Fred had better give you an order for a thousand meters!" How we got out of his office without collapsing I don't remember, but as soon as Fred Prince, Herb and I could get over to Heublein's, I wired Mr. Bunn, and then we did a little celebrating.

As I had promised Mr. Dunham to deliver some meters on the order within three months, and as the drawings for the parts of the type "H" hadn't even been started, it was *very* imperative to work fast, so we hastened home the last week in December, and within ten days, Otis White and I, working frantically, had drawings completed and tool work started. The necessary tools for the entirely new meter were completed by the latter part of January, 1911, faster than we ever did any job before or since, and we shipped the first meter to Hartford on February 5, 1911, well ahead of our promise to Mr. Dunham. Fortunately, it did all we had claimed for it, and thus began our association with the Hartford Electric Light Company, which has continued unbroken ever since, a record of which we are very proud.

Compensation of induction meters. Arrangement with Westinghouse under Shallenberger patent— Spring of 1911.

ON account of the Shallenberger patents of the Westinghouse Company, covering the method of obtaining quadrature of the shunt field in an induction meter, which would not expire until October, 1912, we were obliged to build these early type H meters without compensation for inductive load accuracy, but we put on the shunt magnet, from the very first, a winding arranged to be closed, so that these meters could be readily compensated by the customer, but were careful to put on each meter a tag stating that compensation should not be effected until after October, 1912, in order to avoid patent infringement.

The Westinghouse Company soon claimed that this was a subterfuge, and threatened to sue us, so in May 1911 I went to New York to see Mr. Charles A. Terry, Vice President in charge of patent matters, who was very fair and reasonable, and soon told me they were willing to license us under the Shallenberger patents, at a royalty that I considered entirely fair, and so reported to Mr. Bunn. After a little further discussion, Mr. Terry and I agreed on a lump sum, to be paid at once, covering the royalty on our estimated production of meters to October, 1912, when the Shallenberger patents would expire, and including polyphase meters, which we could not have made unless compensated. So the money was paid, and the next week we began shipping compensated singlephase meters, and immediately started on the design of our first polyphase meter, under the direction of Jacob W. Bard, who had come with us from the Peoria Electric Light Company in April, 1911, to develop an engineering department. The first polyphase meters were completed and shipments started in the early fall of 1911, essentially the same in design as our two disk polyphase of today.

WHILE we were thus so occupied with the type "H" development, other interesting and important matters came up in the fall of 1910 to tax our development and manufacturing facilities, the first being concerned with Mr. Warren Noble, whom Barela Southwick, then one of our principal and most energetic salesmen, had met in Detroit in September. Noble, one of the most brilliant and interesting men it has ever been my fortune to meet, had come to this country from England in 1906, a very young man, but even then with extensive experience in motor car design, and, after being connected with several companies, had gone with Mr. Walter Flanders in the summer of 1910 to develop a radically new type of electric pleasure vehicle.

Warren Noble. —Development of distant dial amperehour meter—1911.

He heard of our ampere-hour meters, and decided he must use them in his new cars, so after a preliminary talk with Southwick, came breezing down to Springfield, and soon had all of us, from Mr. Bunn down, completely "sold" on his ideas, and especially, on the *very* special and expensive amperehour meter he wanted us to get up for him. His idea was to have the meter proper concealed down under the seat, and arranged with contacts to operate a separate dial mechanism located on the steering arm column of the car. It sounded simple enough, but before we got what Noble wanted, what a headache *we* had!

For three or four months that fall of 1910 Otis White, Carl Struck and I worked four or five nights a week, trying to get up a contact mechanism that would meet the severe requirements put on it, and a corresponding dependable dial mechanism. We finally developed schemes, largely due to Carl Struck's ingenuity (as shown so frequently in all the years since) for these devices that worked, although some slight changes in details were made later, and early in 1911, delivered the first distant dial meters to Flanders. For a year this business looked very promising, but the Flanders design and sales plans were too advanced and ambitious, so it all "folded up." However, other manufacturers of electric pleasure vehicles, such as Woods, Rauch and Lang, and Anderson, became interested in the distant dial meter A particularly interesting type was developed for Woods, in which a Weston ammeter and the distant dial were housed in an oblong case.

JUST after we had gotten well started on the distant dial experiments, one day in November, 1910, a tall, lanky, kindly faced man walked into my tiny office, over in the No. 1 building, and said "My name is Kettering, from Dayton. I need an amperehour meter for a job I'm working on, and our mutual friend, Frank Tait (then, as now, President of the Dayton Power and Light Company) told me to come over and see you." Thus began a most interesting and delightful association, which has extended unbroken through this more than a quarter of a century, and has meant to me more of inspiration and high ideals in engineering and research than I have had from any other man No one could have a better friend than I have had in "Ket" since that winter day so many years ago.

He sat down and told me of his association with the National Cash Register Company, and of having quit them a few months before to go with Mr. Edward A. Deeds in organizing the Dayton Engineering Laboratories Company to make ignition systems for motor cars. This had led "Ket" to the conception of an electric starter for motor cars, and when he came to Springfield, he had built some models in Mr. Deeds' barn, near Dayton, and was now trying to get some storage battery manufacturer to have enough faith in his scheme (and in the battery) to supply him the necessary batteries, and was also seeking sources of supply for ignition coils, and for the starter motor and generator.

Mr. Kettering felt it was absolutely essential to

Our first contact with Charles F Kettering — November, 1910.— Development of Delco amperehour meter for Cadillac cars. —April, 1911.

the success of his system to keep the battery fully charged, and also protected against overcharge, so naturally turned to the amperehour meter. At first, his scheme sounded almost fanciful to me, but he soon had me convinced, and in December, 1910, busy though we were on the type "H" development, we succeeded in making two models of an amperehour meter, very different in design from our regular meter, to meet "Delco" requirements, and I took them over to Dayton, where, by this time, "Delco" had a small floor in a downtown building.

These meters, with some slight changes, proved satisfactory, and we thought we might get an order for a few more samples to be tried out with starters on cars, when one day in February, 1911, "Ket" telephoned me to come to Dayton at once, and there he gave his several suppliers the astounding news that Mr. Henry M. Leland, then president of Cadillac Motor Car Company, had decided to put "Delco" starters on *all* Cadillacs, beginning with the "1912" cars to be brought out in July, which meant we must start delivery of Delco meters in Dayton early in May. So, right after our rush to tool up and produce the type "H," we had to start in and do the same thing on the Delco meter. So the next few months were not enjoyable, but we made it, and sold many thousands of meters to Delco that year, still more in 1912, when Hudson, as well as Cadillac, used Delco starters, and then this business ended in 1914, as electric starters had been simplified by that time so that the battery could be protected without an ampere-hour meter, and also, with competition greatly reducing the price of a starter, the meter was too expensive to be used.

HOWEVER, the connection thus started with Mr. Kettering and his company led us the next year, 1914, into a still more important ampere-hour meter business, through the development by them of the famous "Delco-Light" farm lighting plant. For this Ket considered an amperehour meter absolutely essential, but it had to be smaller, more accurate, and less expensive than the "Delco" meter, so, after several months effort, we produced the "MS" meter, soon thereafter adopted by Delco-Light, and later, by practically every manufacturer of farm lighting plants in the United States. This business reached a peak after the war of nearly five hundred "MS" meters per day, then suddenly, in less than two weeks, stopped short when the "farmers' buying strike" came on in September, 1920, and never came back, but it was great while it lasted.

MS ampere-hour meter for Delco-Light plants—1914.

NOW, going back to the fall of 1910, when so many things of importance happened to us, we opened our first branch office, at 50 Church St. New York. Mr. M. B. Chase, whom we met and secured through Herb Young, was appointed district manager, thus taking over the territory formerly handled by Machado and Roller, who had "dropped us" a few

Opening of first district office at New York—December, 1910.

months before. We stayed in this space a few years, then moved to larger quarters higher up in the same building, Mr. Chase continuing with us until succeeded by T. B. Rhodes in 1917.

Advertising arrangement with Ray D. Lillibridge, New York— 1911. IN the spring of 1911, realizing the need of better looking technical bulletins and advertising than we had been able to prepare ourselves, we made an arrangement with Ray D Lillibridge of New York, who had successfully handled the Wagner Electric Company's advertising for several years, and this continued, to our mutual satisfaction, for many years, until Mr. Lillibridge sold his business to his associates, Otis Kenyon and Henry Eckhardt, who continued to handle our account until the depression. The long connection with Mr. and Mrs. Lillibridge (who was most active and successful in the business) and Mr. Kenyon is one of the pleasantest experiences of my years with Sangamo.

Sumner Rogers comes with us as Production Manager— April, 1911 IT was also in the spring of 1911 that Sumner B. Rogers ("Blackie") came with us, after several years at Western Electric Company,—as Production Manager, and so continued until he left for war service in May, 1917—more about him later.

Our order for the great 60,000 ampere shunt—May, 1911. ONE day in May, 1911, I had a telephone call from Omer Brasher, formerly meter superintendent at Galveston, one of the most energetic and determined sales engineers we ever had, who was then travelling in western New York. He said, "Boss,

I'm at Niagara Falls, and have just come from a talk with Mr. John Harper, General Superintendent of Niagara Falls Power Company, and he gave me an order for a 60,000 ampere D-5 meter, so I guess we will have to make it." I nearly collapsed, and told Brasher he was crazy, and ought to be fired, as we had never attempted a shunt for more than 10,000 amperes, and, so far as I knew then (or now) no one had ever tried to build a 60,000 ampere shunt. However, Brasher said we just had to back him up, so I said I would go that night to Niagara Falls, and, on arrival there, found that the big shunt, and two smaller ones (merely 25,000 amperes each) were to be used in measuring energy sold to the Aluminum Company of America for producing the metal Mr. Harper stipulated a lot of conditions as to the shunts and meters, which made the job look even worse, but we tackled it, and came out all right, as the big shunt has been in successful operation now for a quarter century, and we have built many more big ones for the Aluminum Company, including several of 50,000 amperes rating. Brasher never could see why I should have been disturbed about that order!

SOON after the introduction of the ampere-hour meter, the Edison Storage Battery Company manifested a keen interest in it, as it was even more necessary with the Edison nickel-iron battery, owing to its characteristics on charge and discharge, than with lead batteries, where voltage gives a rough idea of the battery condition. Mr. Edison himself was

My first meeting with Mr. Edison through his interest in amperehour meters—1911.

very much pleased with the amperehour meter, and promptly had one put on Mrs. Edison's electric car, and also wrote a number of his friends in this country and abroad, strongly recommending Sangamo meters. One day early in 1911 we had a letter over his own signature saying that the meter on his car needed some repairs, and asking where to send it. At that time we had no service department at New York, so I wrote him to send it to Springfield. He sent it, and asked us to hurry it back, so, as I happened to be going to New York, I took the meter with me to East Orange, and thus met Mr. Edison for the first time. His son Charles took me up to see his father, whom we found in his laboratory, with his head against a phonograph case, for, owing to his deafness, this was the only way by which he could hear, or rather, *sense* records. When his son introduced me as "the fellow who makes those Sangamo meters," Mr. Edison looked up and said, "Young fellow, Mrs. Edison can't run her electric without your meter, so why couldn't you fix it up nearer than out there near Alaska! You must have a service department at New York." So we started one there.

Then followed a most interesting talk about his early work on meters, not only his famous chemical meters, but others with which he had experimented. I went to see him several times in later years, and always found him kindly and interested, but that first meeting with him stands out as one of the great experiences of my life.

BY the spring of 1912, type "H" and ampere-hour meter business had increased to a point where we needed more space, so No. 4 building was erected that summer, and occupied in October, the same month that we formed a sales connection with the Federal Electric Company, of Chicago, which has continued most satisfactorily ever since.

Beginning of our connection with Federal Electric Co. and erection of No. 4 Building— Fall of 1912.

This connection came about through Mr. John F. Gilchrist, Vice President of the Commonwealth Edison Company, one of the finest and truest friends that Sangamo and Mr. Bunn and I personally ever had, following a very satisfactory report to him on type "H" meters from Mr. O. J. Bushnell, to whom I have referred before as our long time critic, friend and advisor.

GOING back to amperehour meters for use with "floating" batteries, as in axle generator train lighting, it was evident, by the spring of 1912, that our field would be greatly limited unless we could find some way of getting the necessary difference in speed on charge and discharge, in a two-binding post meter, in other words, one that could be put in the battery line, and which would automatically go slower on every change from discharge to charge. I had all sorts of schemes, none practical, until one day in May "Dutch" Hodde came to me with a suggestion that Jake Bard and I said wouldn't "work." Dutch didn't say anything more *then*, but one day about a month later he came in and said "I've got a freak meter on the rack out here, and wish you would

The variable resistor for amperehour meters.— Hodde puts one over on me.

come see what's the matter." So when I arrived, here he had an amperehour meter all fixed up according to his scheme, and as he threw the switch back and forth from charge to discharge, and the meter changed speed each time, Dutch grinned, and said, "Well, now, does it work?" Thus was born the "variable resistor," which met every requirement, and which has been so successfully used in every amperehour meter since that time. This experience taught me a lesson about condemning too quickly any engineering suggestion, until thoroughly investigated and tried out.

With the development of the variable resistor, the application of the amperehour meter with axle-generator train lighting equipment became possible, and our success in this field was greatly aided by Edward Wray, who was then editor of the principal technical magazine in this field, and who had become interested in the amperehour meter when it was first announced, following extensive experiments he had made with train lighting equipment while a student at the University of Wisconsin a year or so before. A few years later he came with Sangamo as Assistant General Manager, continuing with us until 1921, when he returned to the field of technical publication, after devoted and successful service to us.

Again Ernest Lunn— ERNEST LUNN, to whom I have referred as the "father of the amperehour meter," left the Commonwealth Edison Company towards the end of

1912, to take charge of car lighting for the Pullman Company, and, following his successful experience of several years with our meters, and now having available the "variable resistor" meter, he recommended to the Pullman officials that these meters be installed on their electric lighted cars, practically all of which were equipped with axle generator devices. They had experienced much trouble with proper charging of the batteries with these equipments, often resulting in loss through too frequent battery renewals, so early in 1913, Mr. Lunn began installing meters on their cars, and during the next two or three years equipped nearly all Pullman cars, then numbering some 6000, with Sangamo meters. He estimated that within two years they thus saved on batteries more than the cost of the meters. In later years, improvements in axle-generator control devices rendered amperehour meters less necessary, but many of them, after more than twenty years, are still in regular use on many Pullman cars, and on other cars of the principal railroad systems.

Amperehour meters for the Pullman Company.

THE spring of 1913 was marked by an event that meant much to Mr. Bunn and me, when we paid Mr. John W. Bunn in full the amounts he had so generously and willingly advanced Sangamo, which enabled us to carry on through the losing years from 1904 to 1911, in which year we at last began to get on our feet financially, and reached a sound condition within another year.

Repayment of loans which carried us through the lean years.

The H-2
meter—1914
First improve-
ment on the
original
type H.

THE next year we brought out the H-2 meter, based on the general design of the original "H," but greatly improved through the inventive genius of Jake Bard, to whose ability and hard work Sangamo owes so much.

Sales arrange-
ments abroad

IN the same year we made one of the most important export connections of our history, when Warburton, Franki & Co., became our agents for Australia, an arrangement which has continued most happily to this day, and which is now about to be further strengthened by Mr. Warburton's decision to undertake the partial manufacture of type "HM" meters at Sydney.

The next year we formed a sales arrangement for Japan with the Ashida Engineering Company of Osaka, and soon afterward Mr. Ken Ashida came over for his first visit with us. This connection continued with mutual friendship and esteem until Mr. Ashida's death in 1927, and his company, now headed by his brother, still continues as our agent in Japan. I shall tell later of our manufacture of meters at the Ashida plant.

Thus, 1915 marked important progress for us in the export field, as 1906, '07 and '12 had in the domestic field and our business with Warburton, Franki and Ashida throughout the years since, testifies to the value of these fine representatives.

IN the spring of 1915, a Capt. Alfred Girard, formerly in the Army medical corps, came to Springfield to visit relatives, bringing with him a small refrigerating machine, for household use, which he had conceived while serving in the Philippine Islands some years before, and had built the model shortly before his visit to Springfield.

Our venture in the domestic refrigeration business— 1915–1919, The Springfield Refrigeration Co.

Mr. Ernest J. Bechtel, Vice President and Chief Engineer of Hodenpyl, Hardy and Co. (now the Commonwealth and Southern Corporation) happened to be in Springfield at that time, so he, Arthur Mackie and I went to see the machine, and were so impressed by its possibilities and "Cap" Girard's enthusiasm that we discussed with other men in Springfield and New York the idea of forming a small company to develop Girard's machine, and shortly thereafter incorporated the Springfield Refrigeration Company.

This company made a contract with Sangamo to do the necessary experimental work, and we started off with high hopes. During the next two years we made many changes and improvements in Girard's original machine, most of this under his direction, retaining, however, ammonia as the refrigerating medium, which was a mistake, as this was never really suitable and safe for a household machine.

After Captain Girard returned to the service in 1917, and as we were very busy during the war, our experiments with the refrigerating machine became very sporadic, and finally in 1919, the Springfield Refrigeration Company "folded up," and Girard took back his patent rights, and built some machines with a company in Chicago. Unfortunately, he was several years too early in this field, especially as the little company we organized did not have a fraction of the capital necessary to carry the machine to commercial success.

Sangamo came out of this undertaking with a considerable loss, but it was valuable experience.

Our exhibit at the Panama-Pacific Exposition, San Francisco—1915. Highest award given us.

OUR first exhibit at a great exposition was at the Panama-Pacific, at San Francisco, in 1915, where we had a very handsome booth, adjacent to our good friends, the Bristol Company of Waterbury. Although neither this, nor subsequent expositions where we have exhibited, were commercially valuable to us, yet we had the satisfaction of receiving at San Francisco the highest award given for devices of the general type that we exhibited. It was during my visit to our exhibit in June, 1915, that I met J. G. Monahan, who some years before had been with the Ferranti Company in Canada, and who had gone to Los Angeles to live, shortly before we met It didn't take us long to make an arrangement for "Jerry" to represent us at Los Angeles, and we have always felt happy over it, as it has proved most satisfactory for both Jerry and us.

Development of Economy street railway meters—Larry Gould—1917

ABOUT this time we became interested in the development of a special type of direct current watthour meter for use on street railway cars, and soon thereafter, arranged with L. E. Gould, of Chicago, a man of long experience in the street railway field, to sell these meters for us. The next year, 1917, "Larry" and we organized a separate company, the "Economy Electric Devices Company," to devote its efforts to the sale of "Economy" meters, and through Larry's ingenuity in adding important features to these meters, and his ability and energy as a salesman, we soon equipped many important street railway systems Eventually, the job was so thoroughly done that most of the important systems in this country, and many in foreign cities, Paris, Rio de Janeiro, Amsterdam, Yokohama, etc., were equipped with these meters, and we found few worlds left to conquer with them. So a few years later we turned the "Economy Electric Devices Company" over to Mr. Gould and some of his associates, who broadened their line to include other devices used by street railways and it so continues to this time.

A S our business thus increased, we again faced the need for more space, so in the spring of 1916 started the erection of No. 5, our main building, which was occupied in October of that year. Then, with further demand imposed by the war, we had the Austin Company erect one of their standard buildings, our No. 6, which was done in record time, as they broke ground early in June, 1917, and we started operations in the building just *six weeks* later !

No. 5 Building erected—1916. No 6 Building —June, 1917.

*Scott Lynn
came with us
1910—Begin-
ning of
Canadian
manufacturing
under him—
1916.*

EARLY in 1910, a young fellow came to us soon after leaving the Naval Academy at Annapolis, Scott Lynn, who soon became one of the most valuable men in our organization, and, after some years in engineering work at Springfield, represented us for a short time at Salt Lake City, his home, and then took charge of our office at Rochester, N. Y. The year after he came with us, and about two years after Mr. Alfred Collyer became our agent for Canada, we organized the Sangamo Electric Company of Canada, Ltd., at that time purely as a selling medium for Canadian business. By 1916, our business there had grown to a point, and Canadian duty restrictions on U. S. meters were such, that Mr. Collyer strongly urged that we begin manufacturing on a limited scale in Canada, so, as Scott Lynn seemed the logical man to take charge of this work, we sent him to Toronto in December, 1916, and the next month started operations in one floor of a loft building on Adelaide Street, West. Under Scott's able direction, our Canadian business rapidly increased, so, within a year, we were obliged to take another floor, and considerably extended the manufacturing work done there, although still supplying many parts from Springfield. By the end of 1918, it was evident that we were in Canada to stay, so, on the urgent recommendation of Mr. Collyer and Scott Lynn, Mr. Bunn went to Toronto and purchased the building at 183 George St. This, extended and enlarged several times in later years, we still occupy.

DURING this period, in 1916, we met Mr. Wm. B. Hale, through Mr. Edward Weston and Mr. Caxton Brown, Mr. Hale having been the Weston representative in Mexico City for some years, and, as Weston and we were anxious to extend our business in Latin American countries, we jointly engaged Mr. Hale, and during that year and 1917, he made a long trip for us to all the countries of South America, developing a lot of new and satisfactory business, especially at Rio de Janeiro, Buenos Aires and Lima.

The Weston Company and Sangamo send W. B. Hale to South America— 1916. Arrangement with Newbery and Rodriguez, Buenos Aires.

Mr. Hale made another trip for us about two years later, and then decided to remain at Rio as our representative, later transferring to Buenos Aires, where he continued as our agent for several years.

Following this, we made an agency arrangement for Argentina with the excellent firm of Newbery and Rodriguez, which was discontinued a few years later, on account of difficult competitive conditions there, but, I am happy to say, was renewed last year (1935) to the satisfaction of both parties.

THE entrance of the United States into the World War brought to us, like all companies of any size, many problems, first, loss of many employes to the service, second, obtaining necessary materials, and third, employes to take the places of those who left. As to materials, we had relatively little trouble, for we were soon placed on the list of preferred industries by the War Industries Board, but it was very

Sangamo's representation in the World War.

difficult to obtain men, and thus became necessary to use women for many jobs formerly performed by men, and it was amazing how well they did such work.

As soon as war was declared in April, 1917, the first to go was our Sales Manager, Barela Southwick, then Captain of Company "C," and soon after Sumner Rogers, our Production Manager, who was a Captain in the Reserve Corps, left, soon followed by Goin Lanphier, our Purchasing Agent, Dana Johnson, Roy Butherus, Donald Funk (who had just come with us from Yale) and many others, so we eventually had a total of 162 in the service, of whom four lost their lives in action, a record of which Sangamo is very proud. Those left at home also had responsibilities in connection with the war, especially our President, Mr. Jacob Bunn, who served as Chairman of the Second District Draft Board, discharging this difficult responsibility with characteristic tact and fairness.

Death of Jacob Bard— December, 1918.—Fred Holtz comes with us soon thereafter. JUST at the end of the war, late in November, 1918, our beloved and brilliant Chief Engineer, Jacob Bard, was taken down with the deadly "flu" then prevailing, and on December 13th passed away, his death following soon after that of George Torzillo, our valued and able sales manager from the fall of 1917.

Bard's loss was a real calamity for us, and I did not see how he could ever be replaced, but Fate intervened, in the rather remarkable way she sometimes does, and we got Fred Holtz, who came with us early in January, 1919. Mr. Bunn and I had met Fred in 1916, through our good friend, Mr. Henry Babson, of Chicago, when Fred was Associate Professor of Electrical Engineering at the University of Nebraska, to which he had recently returned after several years' valuable experience with the General Electric Company at Schenectady, and especially with Dr. Steinmetz.

We were then anxious to have him come with us, as assistant to Jake Bard, but before our discussion reached a conclusion, we were in the war, and Fred entered the service, ending in November, 1918, as Captain in the Signal Corps. So, knowing he would soon be out of the service, he wrote me the *very week* that Jacob Bard died, asking whether we would have an opening for him, so, the day after Jacob's death, I wired him to come to Springfield, which he did, and, after a very short talk with Mr. Bunn and me, decided to come with us. We secured his early release from the service, and he thus came with us to begin the organization and development of a full-fledged engineering department, which has been responsible, more than any other factor, for our success in the years since 1919.

RIGHT after this we received a letter from Mr. Charles Hunter, Managing Director of the Edison-Swan Electric Company, Ltd., of London, saying he had heard of our meters through a mutual friend, and as their arrangement for the sale of a

Our connection with Edison-Swan Electric Co. Ltd. of London—1919. My trip to England that summer

well-known English meter had recently been terminated, they wanted an arrangement with us for the British Isles and Australia. Following our favorable reply, "Ediswan" sent over one of their directors, Mr. Edward Gimingham, who had been associated in "Ediswan" with Sir Joseph Swan and Mr. Edison, almost from its inception in the late '70s, to negotiate a contract with us, and he stayed in Springfield several weeks in February, 1919. Mr. Bunn then decided that I should go to England to further investigate this very important matter, before concluding an agreement with "Ediswan," so in April, shortly after Mr. Gimingham's return, I went over, remaining nearly four months to work out an arrangement, and to visit our agents in Barcelona, Paris, Milan, Brussels and The Hague. After much cabling and writing to Mr. Bunn, he finally approved a contract with "Ediswan," for an initial period of ten years, under which we gave them our exclusive agency for the British Isles and India, and non-exclusive for Australia, the latter being made possible only through the courtesy of Mr. Warburton, who kindly waived his exclusive agency for Australia (which he has again had since 1933) to enable us to make a deal with "Ediswan" Under this contract, "Ediswan" agreed to erect a building for us at the west side of their works at Ponders End, Middlesex, which was started that fall, and finished early in 1920, and to undertake an active sales campaign on Sangamo meters in Great Britain As a first step in this, I visited most of their depots in England and

Scotland during June, 1919, being most courteously received by their depot managers and salesmen, and the high light of the trip was when I went with Mr. Hall, of their Glasgow depot (now, I am glad to say, with British Sangamo) and obtained a fine order from the Clyde Valley Electric Company, "Ediswan's" first Sangamo business. I am happy to say that Clyde Valley Company has continued ever since as one of the most important of our customers in the British Isles.

Also, during this trip to Scotland, while going from Glasgow to Edinburgh with Hall, I had a brainstorm which resulted in our K.V.A. meter, a new conception, I believe, in measuring and recording the energy, wattless energy, and varying power factor of a polyphase circuit.

DURING my visit to Paris in May, I met M. Albert Delamare, for many years before representing Landis and Gyr in Paris, and made arrangements with him to represent us in France. Following this, Mme. Delamare and he visited Springfield the following winter, and when they returned to France, he started energetically and successfully to develop business for us there, but after a year or so, the increasing restrictions of the French government on importation of foreign meters made it practically impossible to continue selling in France, so in July, 1921, we had to discontinue our arrangement with M. Delamare, to our great regret.

Arrangement with M. Delamare.— We open our office in Paris —1920.

IN February, 1919, Sumner Rogers returned from the service, and, anticipating an arrangement with "Ediswan," we decided to send him to England to take charge of our venture there, but, in preparation, decided to have him make a trip to Japan, Australia, New Zealand, and the East Indies, to acquire a first hand knowledge of the market for meters in those countries, and to assist Mr. Ashida in determining further expansion of our activities in Japan. Rogers had a very interesting and successful trip of ten months, from May, 1919 to March, 1920, and late that fall, went to England. In the meantime, after considering the organization of a British company jointly with "Ediswan," we had decided to own it entirely, so, early in 1920, British Sangamo Company, Ltd., came into being, and soon afterward, in February, we sent Roy Butherus to Ponders End to get our testing equipment installed in the new building, and to start preliminary manufacturing, mostly with parts sent from Springfield. Roy had come with us, as a very young lad, in 1912, and after several years in the factory and testing room, went into the service, gaining valuable experience in the Signal Corps. After his return from France, he was again in the testing room, and, when we looked around for a capable young fellow to send to England, to take charge of assembling and testing, "Dutch" Hodde selected Roy, and we have had every reason, in the years since, to congratulate ourselves on this happy choice.

Later, Roy became Secretary, Chief Engineer and

Superintendent of British Sangamo, but, eventually, as the business grew, devoted himself entirely to the two first duties, and to him, our great success in England in using Bakelite, and the development of our prepayment mechanism, are due.

Actual production at the British plant was considerably delayed for various reasons, but finally got under way in April, 1921.

DURING my visit to Barcelona, in May, 1919, I visited the Ebro Power Company, a subsidiary of the Canadian and General Finance Corporation, and found them interested in our A.C. meters, but also anxious to obtain a D.C. amperehour meter for house service, a purpose for which our mercury meter was not acceptable to them. They were therefore using a European make of commutator type amperehour meter, and, after examining this, I rashly said we could make a better one, at a competitive price, so Ebro gave us an initial order for 1000 of the proposed meter. On my return home, I put the problem up to Fred Holtz, and we soon designed a meter, called the "LC," and during the summer of 1920, shipped the first order, and more, to Barcelona. But this job was just grief from the start,—for the engineering department, for the factory, and, worst of all, for our customer, so, after expensive effort to get these meters right, and finding their cost prohibitive as compared with the price we could get for them, we gave up this venture, and wrote off a large loss to experience.

My trip to Barcelona—May, 1919—The LC amperehour meter.

Acquirement of ground and buildings from Illinois Watch Co — January, 1920

JANUARY, 1920, marked a great step in Sangamo history, when we bought from the Watch Company the land and buildings they had rented to us up to then. This transaction was financed by a bond issue to the Watch Company, and the early retirement of this obligation, within three years, was largely due to the excellent financial guidance of Mr. J. H. Holbrook. He had returned to Springfield, after several years with the National City Bank, of New York, in July 1920, to become Vice President of the Springfield Marine Bank, and, at the same time, a Director, and Treasurer of Sangamo, and continued in those capacities most successfully until his death in June, 1935.

No. 7 Building erected—1920

DURING 1919, our business at Springfield increased so rapidly that we required more space, so had the Austin Company erect No. 7 building, which was occupied in 1920 by the assembling, testing, and shipping departments.

Our manufacturing venture with Ashida in Japan.—Dana Johnson takes charge there—1920.

AS a result of Rogers' long visit to Japan in 1919, and at the urgent request of Mr. Ashida, we decided to join with him in the manufacture of meters at Osaka, under an arrangement for sale of parts to him, plus certain royalties, while he planned to make bases, grids, covers, series coils and some other parts, and do the assembling and testing operations. It was evidently necessary to send a competent man from Springfield to take charge of this work, and again Hodde selected a man from his department, Dana Johnson, who had also returned from the service in 1919. So Dana went to Osaka in the Fall of 1920, and as a first step, learned Japanese, so that he was soon able to assist Ashida in his sales work in Japan and Manchuria, as well as managing the manufacture of meters. He was very successful in his work, as evidenced by the rapid growth of our Japanese business for several years, but, following the great earthquake in 1923, there was such an enormous demand for meters in Japan that several European manufacturers rushed in and offered destructive prices, with the result that we decided, early in 1928, to withdraw Johnson from Japan, and he returned home in July, to take charge of our Lincoln meter business, as related further on. However, we continued our arrangement with the Ashida Company, which still manufactures Sangamo meters, some parts still being supplied by us and Canadian Sangamo, but most of the meter now being made in Osaka.

EARLY in 1921 our Engineering Department developed the type "N" amperehour meter, doing away with the damping disk and separate damping magnets of the long-established D-5 amperehour meter and giving a much more rugged construction for the severe service to which battery meters are subjected. The "N" construction has been successfully used ever since, both at Springfield and at British Sangamo.

Development of the type N amperehour meter—1921.

Mr. Bunn and I visit our British factory and the Continent—Spring of 1921.

EARLY in 1921, Rogers had some serious problems, both as to manufacturing, and our contract with "Ediswan," so, in February, Mr. Bunn and I went over, and determined on considerable additions to our then very meager facilities at Ponders End, and also adjusted certain features of our contract with Mr. Ford, Chairman of "Ediswan." We also visited M. Delamare in Paris, and our agent in Milan, our business in Italy then being quite important, though later brought to an end by the low-price competition of Italian and German meter manufacturers.

Production of moving picture, "Story of an Electric Meter"—1921

THAT spring we engaged the Rothacker Film Company of Chicago, to produce a three-reel moving picture of our product and manufacturing operations, entitled, "The Story of an Electric Meter," one of the earliest of the industrial pictures produced in co-operation with the U.S Department of Commerce, and the Bureau of Mines. The film was very successful, and having been first heartily approved by Mr. Hoover, then Secretary of the Department of Commerce, it was first released at the N.E.L.A. Convention at Atlantic City, in May, 1921, where it attracted such favorable comment that it was soon in great demand in this country and abroad, so that eventually some twenty copies were in circulation. During the eight or nine years that it continued to be shown, we estimated that over a million persons saw our "movie," so it was a good advertising investment for us.

AS far back as 1914, we had been interested in the production of a demand attachment, having made an arrangement at that time with the Minerallac Electric Company of Chicago to manufacture their attachment, which was one of the first, if not the first, on the U. S. market, having been manufactured by them for several years. Their Chief Engineer, Mr. Chester I. Hall, therefore came to Springfield, where he spent much time for the next year or so with Jake Bard, improving the attachment, and supervising our manufacture of it. Unfortunately, just as we were well launched on this enterprise, the Minerallac Company was taken over by General Electric, and the production of these demand attachments was transferred to Fort Wayne, Mr. Hall also going with G. E., where he later developed many important devices in the demand metering field, especially the "Graphometer" and "Printometer." Through the courtesy and fairness of Mr. Fred Hunting, then head of the G. E. Fort Wayne works, and my good friend of many years, all of our material in process, tools and other items, for the production of Minerallac attachments, were taken over at a price that let us out without any loss on the undertaking, but we were thus left without any demand device. So, during the next two years, Jake Bard gave such time as he could to the problem of developing demand devices of our own, and built several very interesting models of graphic demand meters. However, with his death, no further work was done until late in 1919, at which time Fred

Our first effort with demand attachments. Minerallac Electric Co. Chester I. Hall —1914–1915.

Holtz and Jim Martin began the development of an attachment, and especially of a small synchronous motor for the timing element, which resulted in the famous Holtz patent application on our type "A" induction-reaction motor in 1921, and the production of the first type "H" demand attachment, embodying this motor, in the summer of 1923. The patent on this motor was finally granted ten years later, after a long interference declared by the patent office, and while other small synchronous motors, operating on different principles, such as our types "F" and "G," have been developed in later years, none, to us, has been so interesting as the type "A," still used, with very slight mechanical changes from the original, in our demand attachments and combination time-switch meters.

Development of the S-2 meter for export trade —1923. IN 1923, recognizing the need for a smaller and less expensive A.C. meter than the type "H," for export trade, we designed the "S-2," which was thereupon produced at our Canadian and English factories, being superseded a few years later by the "S-3," similar in design, but improved in structure and performance. Manufacture of this meter was discontinued at British Sangamo early in 1928, but still continues as a very important part of our Canadian company's business, through whose engineering department also came the development of the "S-3" polyphase, and combination of the "S-3" with Lincoln demand elements, in the years between 1925 and 1930.

IN January 1924 Mr. Rogers cabled us of serious difficulties at British Sangamo in connection with a large order from Australia, which had come just at a time when the very existence of our British company was threatened through a combination of circumstances, so Mr. Bunn told me to go to England at once, and I arrived at Ponders End early in February. Within a short time we had worked out a program, and by the time I returned, early in May, British Sangamo was out of the woods, and on the successful upward course it has maintained since, principally due to the good business judgment and firmness shown by Rogers in this crisis, and the engineering ability of Roy Butherus. *Second visit to British factory— January, 1924.*

IT was also about this time that our British company began to enjoy the splendid business relations with the North Metropolitan Electric Supply Company, of Middlesex County, that have continued ever since, and thus to the personal relations with their Chief Meter Engineer, George F. Shotter, one of the leading authorities on meters in Great Britain, whose wise and unselfish advice and suggestions have contributed so much to the success of British Sangamo. *Our relations with North Metropolitan Electric Supply Co.—George F. Shotter.*

DURING this trip I visited several of our agents on the Continent, but the outstanding event of the trip was my first meeting with the famous Italian scientist and engineer, Dr Guido Semenza, of Milan, to whom I had a letter of introduction from his life *My friendship with Dr. Guido Semenza, of Milan.*

long friend, Mr. John W. Lieb, Vice President and General Manager of the New York Edison Company. Dr. Semenza was then, and until his untimely death in 1931, the Chairman of the International Electro-Technical Commission, head of the C. G. S. Meter and Instrument Company of Monza, near Milan, and one of the three greatest electrical engineers in Italy. He was a simple, kindly man, and I shall never forget the courtesies of himself and his family to us on this, and a subsequent trip to Italy in 1927. In the meantime, he honored us with a visit to Springfield in 1926, and expressed much pleasure in seeing our factory and laboratory.

Our venture in the electric clock business, beginning 1926. —Hamilton-Sangamo Co — 1929 —Sale of business to General Time Instruments Corporation— 1931.

AND now I come to the most important venture in which Sangamo ever engaged, outside of the meter business—electric clocks In the winter of 1923–24 Fred Holtz was in Europe investigating new developments and assisting our British factory, and, hearing a lot about several new types of electric clocks then being offered in England and on the Continent, he thought of using our little type "A" motor to wind the spring of a clock, not a new conception, fundamentally, but his idea was new in respect to several important features. On his return, he discussed his scheme with Mr. Bunn and me, and it sounded so good that Mr. Bunn asked him to build some models for which the Watch Company supplied movements. During the latter part of 1924 we built some forty clocks, which gave such good results over a period of several months that we decided to engage in the manufacture of these clocks, and, after tooling up the following year, produced the first clocks in the spring of 1926, shortly before Mr. Bunn's death. Regular production of a handsome line of clocks, with several styles of cases made by Erskine-Danforth, was started that summer, and in October we announced these clocks to the trade.

At this time, synchronous clocks had not been generally accepted, as they were later, so our new line was favorably received by jewellers throughout the country, and we then started a very ambitious and expensive campaign of advertising of our clocks, both in trade and popular magazines. Early in 1928, the Hamilton Watch Company had purchased the Illinois Watch Company, and began operating the Springfield plant. Through our association with them, especially in the purchase of 11-jewel escapements for our clock movements, the suggestion was made in September, 1928, by Mr. Charles F. Miller, President of Hamilton, that we join forces in the electric clock business, resulting in organization, on June 1, 1929, of the Hamilton-Sangamo Corporation, equally owned by the two companies. The plan was for Sangamo to continue manufacture of the clocks, with Hamilton supplying the escapements and the sales experience.

Under this impetus, the new company started with bright prospects, but already the greatly increased vogue of synchronous clocks, at far lower prices than those at which we could sell our electrically wound clocks, was giving us difficult competition, and when the crash in all business started in October, '29, the problems of Hamilton-Sangamo became still more difficult. To meet the synchronous clock competition we therefore developed our type "E" non self-starting synchronous motor during the spring of 1930, and in August put on the market a new line of clocks embodying these motors, which were favorably received. However, we soon realized that we needed a self-starting synchronous clock, so later that year produced the first type "F" self-starting motor, principally due to the engineering ability of one of our principal research engineers, Fritz Kurz. We were about to offer a line of self-starting clocks embodying this motor, when, in December, 1930, the General Time Instruments Corporation of New York, owning the Western Clock Company ("Big Ben") and the Seth Thomas Clock Company expressed an interest in using the type "F" motor in their electric clocks. As we could not sell motors to any other concern than Hamilton-Sangamo, the upshot of the matter was that Mr. Ralph Matthiessen, President of G. T. I. Corporation, offered to buy the Hamilton-Sangamo Corporation, and thus obtain the exclusive rights to the use of all our motors, A.C. and D.C., for clock purposes, as well as the established business of the Hamilton-Sangamo Corporation. The business was therefore sold to G. T. I. Corporation in April, 1931, and Hamilton and Sangamo retired from the clock business, with considerable loss, but with much valuable experience.

SHORTLY after Mr. Holtz and I returned from Europe, in the spring of 1924, we realized the inadequacy of our engineering and research facilities, so, with some hesitation, presented to Mr. Bunn our plans for a really complete and well-equipped laboratory. To our great satisfaction he immediately said he agreed with us, and to go ahead, so our present laboratory was built that summer, and occupied that Fall; it has paid for itself many times over since then.

Research Laboratory built—1924.

IN the spring of 1924 our New York manager at that time, T. B. Rhodes, met a former army engineer named Pressley, who had recently invented a new radio "hook-up," involving the use of the super-heterodyne circuit. At that time radio sets were being largely built by amateurs from sets of parts, tuning coils, transformers, condensers, chokes, etc., so Pressley planned to offer a set of transformers and fixed condensers to enable amateurs to employ his circuit As he was well vouched for, and as his circuit was very good, we made a royalty arrangement with him, and in September 1924, put the "Pressley kit" on the market. It met with instant favor, but our success was short lived, for in December the Radio Corporation of America notified us that the Pressley circuit infringed some of their most important patents, so, on advice of our counsel, we discontinued manufacture of the Pressley parts in January, 1925.

Our venture in the radio parts business. Pressley circuit—1924.— Experiments with receiving sets—1925-27.

However, in developing these parts we had made a very satisfactory fixed condenser molded in Bakelite, the first, I believe of this type, so we immediately followed the Pressley kit with our type "A" condenser, which, later, was supplemented by the cheaper "Illini" type, and both were successful.

During the great boom in production of radio sets in 1928–29, our sale of these condensers to manufacturers of receiving sets was very large, but with the crash this business dropped off sharply However, the type "A" condenser still continues to be favored for use in important radio devices, and several other types are also now made by Sangamo.

Soon after the introduction of these condensers, in 1925, we learned of a very fine receiving set which had been developed by a group in the East, including some of our business friends, and for which license rights were being granted to a small group of well-known manufacturers. We decided to take a license, and then undertook development of a fine set, which we proposed to sell at about $600. We built nine sets, after much preliminary experimental work, at a cost of some $25,000.00, which were put in service early in 1927, and gave splendid results, but by this time, with the clock venture requiring large expenditure, we realized that we could not go on with radio sets except at great expense and at the risk of jeopardizing our meter business, so in 1928 the radio set project was dropped.

IN September, 1925, I had to go to California on business with Jerry Monahan and Lorrin Nott, so Mr. Bunn, Mr. Henry Merriam and Mr. Arthur Mackie decided to go along, as they said, to "check up" on me. We had a very interesting and enjoyable trip, until we reached the Grand Canyon, on our return, where Mr. Bunn became ill, but we thought it was only a cold. However, on our arrival home the middle of October, he was still sick, and then began the long illness, culminating with the greatest blow that has ever fallen on Sangamo, when Jacob Bunn passed away on May tenth, 1926. *Mr. Jacob Bunn's death —May 10, 1926*

For nearly thirty years I had been so closely associated with him, and had received from him all those years such unfailing interest, sympathy and understanding of our problems, that his going meant to Sangamo and to me a great void which could never be filled. Since his death, all of us associated with him have tried to carry on as we felt he would have wished us to, so whatever Sangamo is today is a monument to its founder and guiding spirit for so many years, Jacob Bunn.

IN 1926, we had our second exhibit at a great exposition, the Sesqui-Centennial at Philadelphia, where, again our products, meters and electric clocks, received highest awards, but this exposition was not so well attended as had been anticipated, and our participation in it was not of great sales value. *Our exhibit at Sesqui-Centennial Exposition, Philadelphia —1926.*

*Sangamo
becomes a pub-
lic company
Listed on
Chicago Stock
Exchange—
June, 1927*

SHORTLY after Mr. Bunn's death, we were approached by Paul H. Davis & Company of Chicago, and Kissel, Kinnicutt and Company of New York, with regard to making Sangamo a public company, and listing our stock on the Chicago Stock Exchange, so in June, 1927, several of the larger owners of Sangamo sold a considerable part of their holdings, and the company was recapitalized with 125,000 shares of common stock, with par value of $16.00 per share, and 10,000 shares of 7% Preferred stock, with par value of $100.00 per share. A large block of both stocks was then offered to the public, in July, 1927, and was quickly taken up. Following this, Mr. H I. Markham, partner in Paul Davis & Company, and Mr. Walter Robbins, then a partner in Kissel, Kinnicutt and Company became directors of Sangamo, our Board being increased to nine members, and both of them have continued to render most valuable service to us since that time.

*Purchase of
land for
British-
Sangamo plant
near Enfield—
Summer of
1927 First
building
erected—1928.
Termination
Ediswan sales
arrangement—
1933*

BY the end of 1926, British Sangamo had outgrown the building at the "Ediswan" works, at Ponders End, so in the summer of 1927, while I was in England, Mr. Rogers and I found a well located piece of land on the Cambridge Arterial Road, just outside of Enfield, one of the important manufacturing suburbs, twelve miles north of London.

During 1928 we erected the first building of the present British Sangamo plant, which was occupied in the summer, and, as the new plant was only three miles from the old factory at Ponders End, we were able to retain nearly all of our employes at the old plant. By this time, Mr. Rogers had decided to confine his meter production entirely to our type "H," so manufacture of the type "S-2" in England was discontinued in the fall of 1928.

From 1926, we had had several discussions with "Ediswan" in regard to modifications of our sales agreement with them, and, failing to reach a satisfactory understanding when the original contract with them expired in 1929, we thereafter continued with them on a temporary arrangement, until we found, early in 1933, that British Sangamo could not develop as it should without control of sales being in its own hands. So, on July 1, 1933, "Ediswan" ceased to represent British Sangamo, and Mr. Eric Dymond, who had been our sales engineer for several years, became Sales Manager of the company, and rapidly organized an efficient sales organization, as evidenced by the fact that the business of our British Company has almost doubled in the three years since we took over our sales. Since 1928 there have only been two years when British Sangamo did not erect additional buildings, the largest additions, in space and equipment, having been made in 1935 and this year, so the plant is now one of the largest and best equipped for meter and time switch manufacturing in the British Isles.

I N February, 1928, we purchased the six acre tract across Converse Avenue from our main building, and that spring erected our No. 1 Warehouse, as our

Purchase tract north side Converse Avenue. Erection No. 1 Warehouse— February, 1928.

space for raw materials and finished stock had become entirely inadequate, and again this spring (1936) we built, adjacent to this, the No. 2 warehouse.

Improvements in construction type "H" meter —From 1914 to 1933. GOING back in history of the type "H" meter, our principal product for the past quarter century, it is a matter of great pride to Sangamo that this meter has been essentially the same in principle and construction for a quarter of a century, the original design having been so well adapted to detail improvements and modifications, as the metering art progressed, that we have found it unnecessary to bring out an entirely new type of A.C. meter in all these years.

In 1914 the original "H" was slightly modified in the electromagnetic structure, and then brought out as the "H-2," then, some fourteen years later, compensation for temperature and overload were incorporated, and the designation (in the United States and Canada) changed to HC, this having been announced in January, 1928

Finally, when the four U. S. meter manufacturers, in 1933, agreed on standardization of external features of all meters, further detail changes were made, resulting in the present HFA and HFS meters, but they can be recognized at a glance as "grown-up" brothers of the old "H" meter of 1911.

Beginning electric time switch business —1930.— Arrangement with Venner. IF our electric clock venture was, otherwise, a losing venture, it brought one good result, our decision to go into the time switch business. We began to consider this in the Fall of 1928, and shortly thereafter, Mr. Charles DeLong, formerly expert designer and model-maker for the Watch Company, showed us the model of an astronomical dial for time switches, some features of which were later incorporated in our present successful design. With this added interest, we hastened the development of a switch embodying our electrically wound clocks, both A.C. and D.C., with 11-jewel escapement made by the Watch Company, which, with almost no changes, still continues as the finest switch in our line, and unsurpassed by any other switch made in this country or abroad. We announced these switches in April, 1930, and in a year from that date, our time switch sales reached the modest volume of about $17,000.00.

Soon thereafter we realized the need of a less expensive line of switches for alternating current, and, as a first step in this direction, we made an arrangement, in January, 1930, with Venner of England, the leading manufacturer of time switches in that country, under which we obtained exclusive rights to their patents, designs, and sales experience for the United States and Canada. However, as our work on the new line of synchronous motor and electrically wound switches progressed, we found it necessary to depart, in many principal respects, from the Venner designs, and the VS and VW, as brought out in the Fall of 1932, therefore embodied many new features, developed in our Engineering department, the most important being the use of a quick break, short gap system, with silver button contacts, which has since proved so successful. Shortly before that time we started the manufacture of our astronomical dial, first applied on our original mercury tube switches, and then on the VS and VW. The other great factor in the success of these switches has been the Type "F" synchronous motor, already referred to.

Organization of Sangamo Fifteen Year Club—1927

IN December, 1927 our "Fifteen Year Club," composed of employes with the three Sangamo companies for fifteen years or more, was organized, and since then has had many enjoyable meetings, with a dinner each December, when new members are taken in and given the much prized membership button, and a picnic for members and their families each summer. Sangamo takes pride in now having over 330 members of the Club at Springfield and 27 more at the Canadian and English plants.

Industrial survey and recommendations of Bigelow Kent, Willard & Co.—1929.

IN 1928, with our largely increased business at Springfield, we felt the need of outside advice on problems of production, handling of material, and costs, so, in September, engaged the well-known firm of industrial engineers, Bigelow, Kent, Willard and Company of Boston to make a preliminary survey of our plant and methods. This was completed and submitted to us in November, and indicated that many improvements, with consequent large savings, besides elimination of production jams in the shop, could be effected at a reasonable cost. So we engaged this firm to undertake the necessary work, to which Mr. Kent gave frequent and able supervision from the beginning of the job, in February 1929, until its completion a year later, but the resident engineer for B. K. W. & Company, Mr. Tarr, deserves the great credit for what was accompolished. During his year with us he planned and installed the conveyor production lines in the Assembling and Testing Department, the conveyor line from No. 11 Department, changed location of many machines to eliminate lost motion, established a new and effective system of production control, and introduced important changes in our cost system.

As a result of this work, we saved the entire cost, including new equipment and machinery installed by Mr. Tarr, and all fees paid to B. K. W. & Company, in less than two years, not to speak of large economies in space utilization.

THE story of Lincoln thermal demand meters, and our relation to them, is an interesting chapter in Sangamo history.

In 1915, our friends Col. E. A. Deeds, and Mr. Kettering, told me that their friend, Mr. Paul M. Lincoln, whom Col. Deeds had known during the early days of the Niagara Falls Power Company, when Mr. Lincoln was in charge of Westinghouse work there, had told them of an idea he had for a demand meter entirely different in principle from any other then used.

Owing to the fact that the meter engineers of Westinghouse, of which Mr. Lincoln was chief power

The Lincoln thermal demand meter and our association with it, beginning 1915.

engineer, did not seem interested in his invention, he decided to have it developed elsewhere, so, at the suggestion of Col. Deeds, I met Mr. Lincoln in Dayton, and soon agreed to interest ourselves in his device. We finished the first model in September of that year, at which time Mr. Lincoln left the Westinghouse Company in order to devote his time to the commercial development of his meter, and the next month presented his first A. I. E. E. paper on thermal demand meters at an Institute meeting in New York, and exhibited the model we had made.

Following this, we were making plans to go ahead promptly under a verbal understanding we had with Mr. Lincoln, when I received a message from Mr. E. M. Herr, President of Westinghouse, asking me to meet him in Chicago, to discuss the Lincoln matter. He then explained to me that he was very anxious to have Mr. Lincoln return to Westinghouse, and had promised him that if he did they would build his meters. However, Mr. Lincoln, with a very high sense of honor, though not obligated to Sangamo by contract, refused to break his understanding with us, unless with our full consent and approval. Of course I told Mr. Herr that we did not want to stand in the way of what was best for Mr. Lincoln, and would consider our understanding with him cancelled, so, immediately thereafter Mr. Lincoln returned to Westinghouse, and in due course, they put his demand meters on the market, but made little effort to push them, at least, so Mr. Lincoln felt.

The United States having then entered the war,

little was done with Lincoln meters for a few years, but, in 1920, Mr. Lincoln having finally severed his connection with Westinghouse, and being unable at that time, under his contract with them on his thermal meter, to build them himself in the U. S., went to Canada, and organized the Lincoln Meter Co. Ltd , at Toronto.

He was fortunate in associating with him in this enterprise Mr. Stanley L. B. Lines, formerly with the well-known English meter firm, Chamberlain & Hookham. While Mr. Lincoln did not go to Toronto to live, he spent much time in Canada, and through the energetic and successful work of him and Mr. Lines, the Lincoln thermal meter, within a few years, became the standard demand device in Canada, and so continues to this time.

After a few years, about 1924, the Lincoln Company found a need for a combined energy and demand meter, and, as a result of Sangamo's early association with Mr. Lincoln, naturally turned to our Canadian Company to obtain the necessary watthour meter elements. The new instruments were thus announced and sold as Lincoln-Sangamo meters, and being eventually developed in many combinations, both singlephase and polyphase, found ready and wide acceptance in Canada and many foreign countries.

As a result of the close and friendly connection between the two companies, and, following several large orders for Lincoln demand meters from the Detroit Edison Company, Mr. Lincoln desired again to undertake manufacture of his meters in this country, first, to sell them to Detroit without duty, and, secondly, to develop other business in the U.S., where up to this time, the block-interval type of demand meters had been used almost exclusively.

Organization of Lincoln Meter Company, Inc in the United States, July 1928

SO, in July, 1928, the Lincoln Meter Co., Inc., was organized with Mr. Lincoln, as President, holding a controlling interest, and Sangamo a minority, and a contract was made with Sangamo to manufacture Lincoln meters for sale in the United States. Rights for Canada and all foreign countries were retained by the parent Lincoln Company of Toronto.

Under the able sales direction of Dana Johnson, who had recently returned from managing our Japanese venture, the business of the U. S. Lincoln Company rapidly grew, with consequent value to it and to Sangamo.

Sangamo Company Limited acquires Lincoln Meter Co Ltd Toronto—1930

THEN in 1930, it seemed desirable, for many reasons, to consolidate the Lincoln and Sangamo activities in Canada, so, in September of that year, the Lincoln Company, Ltd., became a division of Sangamo Company, Ltd., Mr. Lincoln and Mr. Lines becoming directors, and Mr. Lines also Vice President in charge of Lincoln meter sales, to which duty he gave fully of his ability and enthusiasm His work was, unhappily, terminated by his sudden death the following spring, in April, 1931, a severe blow to our Canadian Company. The Lincoln plant, on Stafford Street, Toronto, was taken over with the business of the Lincoln Company, and continued to be used for production of Lincoln meters to some extent, until this year, but is now exclusively devoted to production of Wagner motors for Canada, as referred to later.

In the fall of 1934, Mr. Lincoln, who had been for a number of years, as now, Director of the Department of Electrical Engineering at Cornell University, expressed a desire to dispose of his interest in the U. S. Lincoln Company, and in December, Sangamo acquired this on a mutually satisfactory basis, since which time the Lincoln Meter Company, Inc., although still retaining its identity, has been operated as a division of Sangamo.

IN June, 1931, when our business at Springfield was beginning to suffer from the depression, we received an unexpected, and very helpful order from the New York Edison Company for 10,000 three-element HC polyphase meters with demand attachments, and some 8,000 clock movements for General Electric, to be used in D.C. demand meters for the Edison Company. These large orders kept us working at top speed until October, and contributed greatly to putting us in sound condition to meet the heavy losses of the next three years.

The big 3-disk meter order from New York Edison— Summer of 1931.

DURING 1931, Mr. Rogers told us that with the greatly increased business of British Sangamo, he felt it necessary to make some major changes in

Changes in organization of British Sangamo— 1932.

his executive setup, so, in October Mr. Funk, our Vice President (and now General Manager), went to England to confer with Mr. Rogers and Mr. Butherus on this matter. As a result of their discussion, it was agreed that Mr. Butherus needed all his time for his heavy duties as Chief Engineer, and should therefore relinquish direction of manufacturing operations. This meant the selection of another man as Works Manager, so, at the suggestion of Scott Lynn, and as approved by Mr. Rogers and Mr. Funk, we sent R. C. Lanphier, Jr. to England in January, 1932, to undertake this responsibility, in which position he has since continued.

Proposed merger — Weston, Bristol and Sangamo — 1929.

FOR many years, as far back as 1915, it had been suggested to us that a merger of Sangamo with certain other companies, and especially the Weston and Bristol instrument companies, might be advantageous, but the matter never reached active consideration until the latter part of 1929, when our friends Kissel, Kinnicutt and Company of New York approached these three companies, and, subsequently, two others in allied lines, in reference to a merger. While we were not especially eager for it, we agreed to submit data, as did Weston and Bristol, and in May, 1930, it seemed that a combination of these companies might be made, but the sudden death of Dr. Wm. H. Bristol, in June, put an end to the negotiations.

OUR acquaintance with Mr. Alfred Collyer began in 1909, through Mr. Walter Robbins,
then Vice President of the Wagner Electric Manufacturing Company of St. Louis, whose products
Mr. Collyer had been selling in Canada for some
time. From then on, Mr. Collyer's principal lines
were Wagner Motors and Transformers, and Sangamo meters, as I have mentioned.

Soon after the war, competition of Canadian made
transformers decreased Mr. Collyer's business in
Wagner transformers, all of which were imported
from St. Louis, and later, as small A.C. motors were
produced in Canada and offered at lower prices, his
motor business, too, was adversely affected, so, during the latter part of 1931 Mr. Collyer decided, with
Mr. Lynn and me, that the best interests of himself,
his sales organization, the Wagner motor business,
and Sangamo would be served by absorbing his organization into Sangamo Company Limited, Mr.
Collyer continuing as Director and Vice President
of Canadian Sangamo, and operating the Montreal
offices. This change was made on January 1, 1932,
and at the same time, our Canadian Company entered into an arrangement with the Wagner Company of St. Louis, under which it acquired exclusive
rights for Canada to the Wagner motor business,
with right to operate this business under the Wagner
Company's name.

Soon thereafter, part of the old Lincoln plant on
Stafford Street, Toronto, was equipped for production of the smaller sizes of Wagner singlephase mo-

Our relations with Mr. Alfred Collyer, beginning 1909.

tors, and part of the motor work was done at the main plant on George Street, but, with increasing motor business, an addition was built at Stafford Street this spring, and all motor manufacturing is now done there.

We go into sign flasher business— 1932.

IN February, 1932, Mr. E. J. Schulenburg came to see us with reference to interesting ourselves in the manufacture of sign flashers, in which business he had been engaged for several years. As this seemed to fit in quite well with our time switch business, we made an arrangement with Mr. Schulenburg, under which we started the manufacture of flashers in a very modest way, but through his energy and knowledge of this business, it soon increased to a point where a separate department was required for the production of flashers.

In the few years since, our Flasher Department has supplied a number of intricate flashers for some of the best known and largest signs in the United States and Canada, especially in New York, Chicago, Toronto, Montreal and Cleveland. This business, started only a few years ago, has thus now become an important feature of Sangamo.

Herbert Nehls comes with us as Export Sales Manager— May, 1932.

IN May, 1932, Mr. Herbert Nehls, who had been a number of years, Sales Manager for North and South America for the well known meter manufacturing firm of Landis & Gyr of Switzerland, came with us as Export Sales Director. Soon thereafter he made a long trip to Cuba, South America and Mexico, followed by further trips to Cuba, Central America and Mexico, and then again in 1935 made a long trip to Europe and South America. Mr. Nehls' efforts so far have been principally beneficial to our Canadian Company, whose S-3 meter has been very popular in the export field, especially in Latin American countries, but his activities now extend in other directions, and he has proved most helpful to the three Sangamo companies.

NINETEEN-THIRTY-TWO is a year that we look back on as a nightmare, for, with the growing force of the depression, our sales that year dropped below one million dollars, and, as a result, our net loss for the year was $268,790.00, a very severe blow to a company of our size. Furthermore, we were distressed through the necessity of laying off so many of our good employes, including many who had been with us for years, and at one time we had less than 500 people at Springfield, most of whom, outside of the offices, were working half time or less. *Effects of the depression — Large loss in 1932*

With 1933 some improvement began and in 1934 we again got slightly on the good side of the ledger.

WHEN the Century of Progress at Chicago was planned, we were somewhat dubious about exhibiting, after our experience at Philadelphia in 1926, but eventually we took a well located space in the Electricity Building and had the most attractive exhibit of the three expositions where we have *Our exhibit. Century of Progress, Chicago — 1933.*

shown. One principal feature of this exhibit was a very large type HC meter, all details being faithful reproductions of the standard meter, and this large meter, arranged to operate on various loads, attracted much attention there, and similar meters, of which we made several, have been used for demonstration purposes by several of our large customers. We also had three large dioramas showing Faraday, Ferraris and Edison, which at the close of the exposition in 1933 were presented to the Julius Rosenwald museum at Jackson Park, Chicago. We derived much satisfaction from having exhibited at this exposition at Chicago, but as it was of little commercial value to us, we did not exhibit the second year.

The standardized "A" and "S" meter program— 1933

AS a result of requests from the Meter Committees of the Edison Association of Illuminating Companies, and of the Edison Electric Institute, the four U. S. meter manufacturers, General Electric, Westinghouse, Duncan and Sangamo, agreed early in 1933 jointly to undertake a program of standardization as to external features of meters, including arrangements of mounting, sealing, etc., and as a result the so-called "A B C" program was started early in 1933. At the same time the socket or plug-in type meter, originally offered by the Westinghouse Company some years before, was made a part of the general program, in other words, two fundamental types of external construction were offered, the "A" or service type meter with improved terminal facilities, and the "S" or socket type meter. This joint program has since been followed in the United States with splendid co-operation between the manufacturers, and with excellent advice and assistance from the two Meter Committees. Through this standardized program the efficiency of metering in the United States has been greatly increased during the past two years.

IN July, 1933, the electrical industry adopted a code under the NRA which was in effect for all electrical manufacturers until the NRA was declared invalid in June, 1935. We did not find the code onerous except for some inconvenience in reducing our normal hours of work to 40 per week, although in principle we had previously believed, and now believe more than ever, that 40 hours should not be exceeded for normal operations of a manufacturing business such as ours With the withdrawal of the code regulations in June, 1935, we therefore continued with these hours for normal operation and there has been no bad effect up to this time, in the way of unfair competition or other practices which were forbidden under the NRA Code. *NRA Code for the electrical industry— July, 1933.*

IN the fall of 1933 our British Company made a very important step in prepayment meters through the introduction of their three-coin meter, the first of this type offered in England, and shortly thereafter introduced a fixed charge collector as a feature of prepayment meters, which has also proved highly *British Sangamo produced three-coin prepayment meters—Fall of 1933 —*

successful. In this connection it is interesting to note
that until very recently our British Company was
the only meter manufacturer in England offering a
full line of meters, both standard singlephase and
prepayment, with Bakelite bases and covers, and our
success in this respect is principally due to the ingenuity and ability of Mr. Butherus in handling
Bakelite for such purposes.

During the early part of 1935 while I was in England, we gave consideration to the matter of changing British Sangamo into a public company and putting some of its stock on the market. After careful
consideration of this problem, we decided in August
to increase the capitalization to 300,000 shares of
common stock, with a par value of 10 shillings each,
and to list the stock on the London Stock Exchange,
which was done in October. At the same time a
large block of the stock was offered to the public
at 21 shillings per share, which was quickly taken
up by stockholders in England and Scotland.
With this change, however, control of British
Sangamo remains with the parent company at
Springfield.

*Service War-
rant plan for
employes
adopted—
December,
1935* DURING the latter part of 1935 we heard of a
plan of extra compensation to employes which
had been adopted several years before by the Pack-
age Machinery Company of Springfield, Mass., and
on investigation of their plan, our directors voted in
December 1935 to adopt a similar plan, of what we
term "service warrants" for all of our employes at

the Springfield plant. Under this plan, after a year's service, an employe receives a warrant entitling him to receive in cash the same amount as paid to stockholders on two shares of common stock. With each year of service an additional warrant is issued, so that an employe with ten years service, for example, now receives under this plan an amount in cash equal to the cash dividend paid on 20 shares of our common stock. This plan was announced the first of this year and was very well received by our employes.

ON January 1st of this year, our company suffered the most severe blow since the death of Mr. Bunn, when Scott Lynn, President of our Canadian Company, died suddenly that evening. The Canadian Company was so entirely his creation and its present position reflects so much his untiring and splendid efforts to build it up, that it will ever remain as a great monument to Scott. Fortunately, and looking forward as he did in every matter, Scott had developed a fine organization, so that Mr. George W. Lawrence, Vice President, assumed the duties of President of the Canadian Company in March of this year, Mr. W. S. Ewens became Vice President in charge of sales, and Mr. D C. Patton, who for many years has been Secretary and Treasurer of the Canadian Company, continued in that capacity. At the same time, the Board of Directors of the Company was strengthened by the addition of Mr. George B. Foster, of Montreal.

Death of Scott Lynn, President of Sangamo Company, Limited— January 1, 1936.

Death of Otis White— May, 1936

MR. OTIS WHITE, our Senior Vice President for many years, and to whom much of the success of Sangamo is due, passed away in May, 1936, after a long and distressing illness. On account of this he had not been actively engaged in his duties with us for several years, but nevertheless his going brought a great sense of loss to those of us who had been associated with him and especially to the writer, after nearly 40 years of the closest and most satisfactory relations with Otis. The present high quality of Sangamo products and the excellence of many of our designs are fundamentally due to Otis White, and as the years go by, Sangamo will never forget what he did for it from the earliest days of the company.

Adoption of vacation pay plan for non-salaried employes— July, 1936

IN June of this year we made a further step in appreciation of the services of our non-salaried employes by adopting a plan of vacation payments, made effective this summer. Under this plan any non-salaried employe with us over three years and less than five, receives three days' vacation with pay, those with us over five and up to ten, one week's vacation, and those with us over ten years, two weeks' vacation with pay. In announcing this plan, which met with highest appreciation from our employes, we stated that should it be necessary at any time on account of business depression to withdraw the plan, such action would apply to salaried as well as non-salaried employes.

FOR some time the directors of Sangamo have been anxious to retire our preferred stock, of which some 7,000 shares were still outstanding at the beginning of 1936. Therefore this spring we decided to offer 2½ shares of common stock in exchange for each share of preferred outstanding, which offer was accepted by a large majority of our preferred stockholders and the stock of those who did not accept the exchange, was purchased on July 1st of this year at the call price of $110.00 per share. As a result of this action the capital stock of this company now consists of only 139,000 shares of common stock, all preferred stock having been retired and cancelled, and the company has no funded debt.

Retirement of our preferred stock—July 1, 1936.

Thus, with the company in strong financial position, with business at the highest point in our history, with splendid relations between our employes and the company, with a commanding position in the fields in which we sell, we can look forward with strong faith and hope to the next forty years of Sangamo, which I hope and believe will be as eventful, interesting and successful as the first forty.

PART TWO

SANGAMO IN PEACE AND WAR
BY
BENJAMIN P. THOMAS

¬»» ¬»» ¬»» ¬»» ¬»» ¬»» ¬»» ¬»» ¬»» ¬»» ¬»» ¬«« ¬«« ¬«« ¬«« ¬«« ¬«« ¬«« ¬«« ¬«« ¬««

II
SANGAMO
IN PEACE AND WAR

¬»» ¬»» ¬»» ¬»» ¬»» ¬»» ¬»» ¬»» ¬»» ¬»» ¬»» ¬«« ¬«« ¬«« ¬«« ¬«« ¬«« ¬«« ¬«« ¬«« ¬««

FOR Robert C. Lanphier, the writing of *Forty Years of Sangamo*, which is reprinted as the first part of this book, was a labor of love, undertaken as a personal memorandum of his experience with Sangamo and as a means of recognizing what others had done in helping to build the company. Four hundred copies were printed and distributed, and almost every copy bore his personal inscription on its fly-leaf. For several years, moreover, Mr. Lanphier had been ill, and perhaps he wished to be certain that the history of Sangamo, as he had known it, would be available to those who would come after him.

DESPITE recurring ill-health, Mr. Lanphier remained active in company affairs almost until his death. During his last years Sangamo continued to expand its plant facilities. A second warehouse and a substantial addition to the tool and die shop were erected in Springfield and many modern machines were installed. In line with his belief that the growth and prosperity of the company must de-

Plant additions in Springfield — 1936 and 1937.

pend largely upon research and experimental development, the space allocated to the engineering department was doubled by the addition of a second story to the building in which it is housed.

Acquisition of Weston Electric Company Limited. IN October, 1936, Sangamo acquired from the Weston Electrical Instrument Corporation of New Jersey a controlling interest in its English subsidiary, Weston Electrical Instrument Company Limited. A manufacturer of ammeters, voltmeters and other indicating instruments, Weston had developed a line of products ideally suited to supplement the meter production of British-Sangamo, and to make possible a considerable diversification of Sangamo's English output. With consummation of the purchase, manufacture of Weston products in England was transferred to Sangamo's Enfield plant, where new buildings were at once put under construction. Within a year Mr. Lanphier was enabled to announce with pride: "It can be truthfully said that British-Sangamo stands first in its field, in plant, in equipment, and in quality and diversity of product."

British-Sangamo changed to Sangamo Weston Limited —1938 WESTON had earned such an enviable reputation in the electrical instrument business that it was thought desirable to retain the Weston name. Consequently, the corporate title of British-Sangamo was changed to Sangamo Weston Limited. The following year Sangamo acquired full ownership and at the same time negotiated a reciprocal engineering agreement with the Weston Electrical Instrument Corporation of America.

SANGAMO'S Canadian business continued to expand, and in 1937, sales of Sangamo Company Limited passed the one million mark. Such rapid development brought need of additional working capital, so the Canadian affiliate sold the parent company 10,000 shares of its common stock at a price of ten dollars a share. *Sangamo Limited prospers.*

SOON after this, Sangamo Electric Company split its own stock two shares for one, so that it now had 300,000 shares of no-par-value common stock authorized with 278,000 shares outstanding. As a further indication of the company's growth, employment reached a new high of 1,475. *Sangamo splits its stock— April, 1937.*

ORGANIZED in 1869, the Illinois Watch Company had progressed from beginnings not much more auspicious than those of Sangamo to a position as a leader in fine watch manufacture whose timepieces were esteemed throughout the world. Sangamo, from the time of its inception, had enjoyed the most cordial relations with the Watch Company. It was Jacob Bunn, president of the Watch Company, who sponsored and encouraged Mr. Lanphier's original experiments with the Gutmann meter, and who, upon the organization of Sangamo, became its president, while at the same time continuing as head of the older company. The *Purchase of the Watch Company buildings— June, 1937.*

Watch Factory had attracted skilled craftsmen to Springfield, and it was from the Watch Company personnel that Sangamo, with the generous cooperation of the Watch Company officials, was able to recruit the key men of its original working force. For the first three years of its corporate existence, Sangamo operated in the Watch Factory, where it was known as "the meter department." The Watch Company built Sangamo's first building for it; and throughout the junior company's developmental years it could always turn to the officials of the older company for guidance and help.

In March, 1928, the Illinois Watch Company was purchased by the Hamilton Watch Company, which operated it as a division in Springfield. During the depression of the 'thirties, Hamilton discontinued its Springfield operations, and in 1937 offered to sell its Springfield property to Sangamo. The proposition was attractive from a long-range point of view and a deal was consummated; and since Sangamo had no immediate need of the buildings it rented space in them to small manufacturing concerns as a means of encouraging industrial development in Springfield.

The tachograph —1937. DURING this year, Mr. Lanphier learned of a new device which had been developed in Germany. Known as a tachograph, it was an instrument designed to reveal the complete performance record of a truck—the distance traveled, its speed at all times, the number and duration of its stops—

by means of a graph drawn upon a circular chart. In an effort to diversify the company's products, Mr. Lanphier obtained the manufacturing rights, imported six or seven of the instruments for experimental purposes, and installed them in trucks. Results were promising, some refinements were worked out, and Sangamo decided to tool up for the production of about 500 tachographs. Further improvements have since been made and the instrument is now one of the company's standard products.

EVER mindful of the welfare of its workers, in 1936 Sangamo instituted a plan of paying Christmas bonuses when business conditions permitted, a practice which it is pleased to have been able to continue ever since. Early to acknowledge the validity of the principle of collective bargaining, in June, 1937, it recognized the Selco Employees Association as the bargaining agency of its workers with respect to wages and working conditions. In the summer of 1938, the company discontinued the Service Warrant Plan, introduced in 1935, in favor of a contributory Pension Plan set up through an arrangement with the Travelers Insurance Company. Based upon sound principles of annuity insurance, it provided for 50–50 contributions by the company and employees and for automatic retirement at age 65.

Employee Relations—1936–1938. The Pension Plan.

Death of Robert
C. Lanphier.

THIS, then, was Sangamo's position at Mr. Lanphier's death, which came on January 29, 1939. His passing marked the end of an era for Sangamo, for he was the last of that illustrious trio of Bunn, Lanphier and White, who had so ably guided the company during its difficult years. The brain and heart of the company since he succeeded Jacob Bunn as president upon the latter's death in 1926, Mr. Lanphier had followed in the traditions of Mr. Bunn's organizational and managerial genius to demonstrate in abundant measure the qualities essential to successful business management. Patient and considerate toward his fellow officers and employees, he had inspired devotion and respect. A pioneer in the field of meter development, his brilliance as an inventor and technician was recognized throughout the engineering world. The city of Springfield mourned his loss no less than Sangamo, for he was active in many movements for civic betterment.

Directors and
Officers—1939.

THE directors elected after Mr Lanphier's death were Mrs. Jacob Bunn, Willard Bunn, Donald S. Funk, J Henry Hodde, Frederick C. Holtz, Mrs. Robert C. Lanphier, Herbert I. Markham, Robert E. Miller and Walter Robbins. Donald S. Funk, who had served as vice-president and general manager, was elected to succeed Mr. Lanphier as president. Re-elected to the offices they had previously held were Mr. Holtz, Charles G. Lanphier and Russell C. Bennett, vice-presidents; George W.

Good, treasurer, and Mr. Hodde, secretary. Robert C. Lanphier, Jr., who had served for eight years as works manager and a director of Sangamo Weston, returned to America to be a vice-president. Later, in June, 1941, Charles R. Horrell was elected a vice-president in charge of sales. The following year, Mr. Good, treasurer for many years, retired because of ill health and was succeeded by Charles H. Lanphier.

THE Lincoln Meter Company, since its organization in 1928, had been operated as a separate corporation, although its product was manufactured at the Sangamo plant with Sangamo equipment. Inasmuch as the Lincoln stock was largely owned by Sangamo, it was thought desirable, from the standpoint of efficiency and economy, to merge the two concerns. Negotiations with the minority stockholders of the Lincoln company were begun at once and within a year the company was taken over by Sangamo and liquidated.

Absorption of the Lincoln Meter Company— 1940.

FOR thirty years, Sangamo's type H meter had proved its all-round excellence, not only by performance, but also by demonstrating its adaptability to all the demands imposed by technological advancement in a highly competitive field. Modified first to compensate for overload, then for variation in temperature, and finally to conform to standardization of electrical connections, it was truly a quality product. Due to the many changes it had under-

The new type J meter—1940.

gone, however, Mr. Lanphier and Mr. Holtz had recognized for some time the need for a new meter and had begun experimental developments as early as 1935. Consequently, a new alternating current, singlephase, watthour meter was now ready for production. Incorporating all the refinements of the old type H meter, whose manufacture was now discontinued, the new meter, designated as type J, was put into production in April of 1940.

The change-over to the new meter necessitated many new departures in manufacturing methods with resultant training of operators in new processes and a short period of manufacturing difficulties such as are inevitably involved in major product changes. There were no serious complications, however, and the new meter soon established a service record that met every expectation.

Sangamo Weston feels the effects of war. WHILE the foregoing developments were taking place in Sangamo, sullen thunderheads of war were thickening over Europe as Adolph Hitler reoccupied the Ruhr and brought Austria and Czechoslovakia under German subjection. In the summer of 1939, Hitler massed 77 German military divisions and 4,000 war planes for a blitzkrieg against Poland; and Great Britain, resolved at last that further German aggression could not be tolerated, was rearming frantically. As early as 1937, British-Sangamo had received government orders requiring increased production of Weston indicating instruments for aircraft and other military apparatus, and in January, 1938, the British company received a contract from the British government to make an improved indicator designed to guide a pilot in making a blind landing in fog.

This led to the development of other special-purpose instruments, and when Hitler struck at Poland, and England declared war on September 3, 1939, Sangamo Weston already had a considerable volume of military business and was prepared to take on more. At the September meeting of the board of directors of the parent company President Funk read a telegram from Sumner B. Rogers, managing director in England, saying that "they had so many things to do that they did not know which proposition to tackle first." The acquisition of Weston Electrical Instrument Limited proved to have been fortunate, as the company now discontinued the production of watthour meters and devoted itself entirely to the manufacture of electrical instruments and accessory equipment, particularly for the Royal Air Force.

The situation of the British plant in the heavily industrialized Enfield district, in North London, put it under hazard of enemy bombing raids and rendered precautionary measures obligatory. Air raid shelters were provided for all employees and the plant was heavily camouflaged.

CANADIAN manufacturers also went on a war footing, and Sangamo Company Limited, at Toronto, began production for military require-

Sangamo Company Limited embarks on war work—1939–1940.

ments. It continued to manufacture a limited quantity of meters, especially for export, but more important was the production of Wagner motors for military and machine tool purposes, pneumatic fittings and gauges for aircraft controls, and radiosondes, a device for recording temperature, humidity and barometric pressure, which was installed in balloons sent aloft for weather predictions.

Further expansion at Springfield— 1939.

MEANWHILE, the only impact of war upon the parent company in the United States was a substantially increased meter business as public utility companies laid in reserve stocks of meters and other essential devices and materials in anticipation of possible later shortages. The directors were concerned with the problems the European war was posing, but none of the difficulties had become critical as yet. A new, single-story building, 200 by 145 feet, with a saw-tooth roof, was constructed at the Springfield plant to permit the more economical processing of raw materials which were formerly passed back and forth between fabricating departments on different levels. The new building also released space to provide more suitable accommodations for the administrative offices.

War threatens the United States—Spring of 1940.

IN the spring of 1940, the dangers inherent in the European situation were brought home to Americans as Hitler ended the quiescent period, known as the "phony" war, by overrunning Norway and Denmark, and pushing with lightning speed through Holland and Belgium to turn the Maginot Line. By the end of June, France was prostrate, and the British Expeditionary Force had barely escaped annihilation at Dunkirk. With Hitler firmly established on Europe's Atlantic coast and apparently preparing for the final stroke at England, the United States was taking belated and urgent measures for national defense. Manufacturers were alerted and urged to find a place for themselves in the defense program.

UNTIL this time, Sangamo, like most other manufacturers of peacetime products, while willing to cooperate with the government, had not been eager for war business. Now, however, the management realized the necessity of helping in the fullest measure possible. Officials of the company made contacts with such agencies as the Chicago Signal Corps Procurement Depot, the Chicago office of Army Ordnance, Wright Field, the Frankford Arsenal at Philadelphia, the Springfield Arsenal and the Washington Navy Yard. Manufacturers in the East and Middle West who already had contracts for war materials were corresponded with or visited with a view to possible subcontracting arrangements which might be adaptable to Sangamo's equipment and personnel. Several possibilities were considered, but for one reason or another none of them materialized. By the year-end, Sangamo had yet to find a place for itself in the ever extending pattern of defense production. Even without mili-

Sangamo seeks a place in the defense program —1940.

tary business, however, sales of the company's products reached a record figure of $5,000,000.

A new plant projected in Canada—1940

FOR several years the directors of the parent company and those of the Canadian subsidiary had recognized the inadequacies of the plant facilities in Canada and from time to time had considered the feasibility of purchasing a new site and erecting a modern plant. Heretofore, the financial position of the Canadian company and the difficulty of disposing of the existing plants had rendered such a move impossible. Now, under the pressure of war, however, manufacturing space in Canada was at a premium and manufacturing plants were readily salable. Accordingly, the Canadian directors authorized the purchase of a new site at Leaside, a suburb of northeast Toronto, and the erection of new buildings, to be followed by the sale of the old properties.

Sangamo Weston is bombed—December, 1940.

AT this time the British plant suffered its first damage from bombs. Bomber attacks were destined to continue almost to the end of the war, but fortunately no serious damage was sustained. There was never a direct hit on the factory, although one bomb struck within eight feet of the building, blowing out the windows, and several others exploded close by. The only casualty occurred one day when a German bomber made a power dive on the plant with two British Spitfires, their machine guns at full chatter, riding hard on his tail. A machine gun bullet clipped the leg of an air raid warden employed by Sangamo, thus giving him the distinction of being the first homeguard casualty in all England.

ON March 3, 1941, Sangamo received its first military business when it signed a contract to convert a number of fire control solenoids for the Navy. This was an extremely simple undertaking, involving merely the winding of new coils and replacement of the old ones in the solenoids. Later in the same month, Sangamo received a small order from the Frankford Arsenal at Philadelphia for the manufacture of $16,000 worth of parts for mechanical time fuzes, a contract that was to give the company no end of trouble. Not only were the manufacturing procedures entirely novel to the company, but it now had its first experience with the rigorous specifications of the military services and with their traditional and often inflexible ways of doing things. Thus Sangamo embarked on war work—a modest beginning, to be sure. But these diminutive initiatory contracts were to be followed soon by larger orders requiring more involved techniques.

Sangamo's first war contracts—1941.

AS the government accelerated the defense program, engineers from the Wright Field Signal Corps Depot, knowing of Sangamo's long experience in the manufacture of fine clocks and time switches, called at the Springfield plant to inquire whether Sangamo could manufacture a precision clock mechanism for regulating the sending of signals from a plane. These signals were to be picked up by ground

The BC-608 contactor—1941

stations whose triangulated arrangement enabled the station operators to determine the plane's position. The mechanism was originally developed by the Royal Air Force, but the U. S. Signal Corps envisioned certain improvements and asked Sangamo to make six models on trial. These were entirely satisfactory, and resulted in the Signal Corps' soon placing a substantial order with Sangamo and authorizing purchase of the necessary tools. New and larger orders for contactors were received from time to time and the company continued to manufacture these instruments until April, 1943.

Indicating instruments for the Royal Air Force BY now, the British company was engulfed in war work, and at the request of the British Air Ministry, Mr. Rogers flew to the United States to discuss with officials of Sangamo and Weston Electrical Instrument Corporation the possibility of those companies manufacturing five selected basic indicating instruments for the Royal Air Force. The purpose of Rogers' trip was to insure an uninterrupted supply of these essential devices in case Sangamo Weston should be bombed out of production in England, for the Luftwaffe was blasting London unmercifully. To assure continued production, such tooling must be done as would make possible the exact duplication of the English-made instruments, including English type threads and other special requirements. A limited quantity of these instruments was produced, but the balance of the order was cancelled when the danger had passed.

ONE of the major accomplishments of the Canadian company during the war was the manufacture of range recorders for the British Admiralty. This instrument was a dual purpose device, whose primary function was to record graphically electrical impulses received from echo ranging underwater sound equipment (ASDIC to the British and SONAR to the U.S.). The recording was performed in such a manner that a time range plot of echoes was provided, the second function of the device being to time, from this record, the release of the depth-bomb barrage in an antisubmarine attack. The Admiralty had approached Sangamo Limited early in 1940 on the subject of making this instrument and shortly thereafter the enormous task of converting the drawings from British standards was launched. It was by far the most complex manufacturing task ever attempted by Sangamo Limited and the redesign and tooling was completed with remarkable dispatch. Instruments were in production by the spring of 1941.

Sangamo Limited and the Range Recorder.

IN midsummer of that year, the United States Navy began negotiations with Sangamo Limited for the purchase of a number of range recorders. Since the Canadian company was already working at the absolute limit of its capacity, it was suggested by George Lawrence, president of Sangamo Limited, that the parent company approach the Navy with the idea of manufacturing the U. S. requirements in Springfield. After three days of discourag-

Entry into the field of Underwater Sound Apparatus— July, 1941.

ing search in the labyrinths of Washington, Sangamo officials located that section of the Bureau of Ships concerned with recorders, only to be informed, however, that the Navy intended to have one of its regular suppliers of underwater sound equipment design and build a recorder superior to the British device. But just as the door seemed about to close on Sangamo, the watthour meter provided the necessary wedge to keep it open. A civilian technician in the underwater sound section had many years earlier been an engineer employed by a competitive watthour meter manufacturer. He told the officer in charge that anyone who could make watthour meters as well as Sangamo could certainly make range recorders. It was then decided that Sangamo should produce at once a model satisfying the U. S requirements. A model, which was fundamentally the British instrument, was quickly put together and tested at sea in late August. In September, a contract for a modest number of instruments was granted. After Pearl Harbor, additional contracts were awarded and eventually Sangamo made many thousands of these instruments. Thus Sangamo Limited's war effort and the excellent reputation earned by Sangamo's watthour meter led to Sangamo's entry into the underwater sound equipment field, an activity in which it has been continuously engaged to the present day.

AS a result of the contact established with the Navy in the manufacture of range recorders, Sangamo was asked to consider the manufacture of a device that would train the crew of a destroyer in antisubmarine operations. The Navy proposed that Sangamo consider making a "Chinese copy" of an equipment developed by the Royal Navy, an extremely complex apparatus involving a multitude of precision mechanical features which represented a hopeless manufacturing task so far as Sangamo was concerned. Again the watthour meter came to the rescue; for, after thorough study, Sangamo proposed to the Navy that the basic design of the equipment be based upon the watthour meter, inasmuch as that instrument, which had already proved its merits in so many instances, would provide for the necessary motion integration in a far more efficient manner than would the various friction drives in the British design. In the device as it was eventually developed a "souped up" J meter element worked fully as effectively as the company engineers had believed it would; and in the further evolution of the attack teacher more watthour meter elements were introduced until, in the final model of the equipment, a total of twenty watthour meter elements were contributing to its successful operation.

Development of the Attack Teacher— October, 1941.

BECAUSE of the defense business upon which it was embarked, Sangamo was required to spend some $50,000 for protective facilities such as wire fence, lights and guard houses around the plant.

The plant protection system.

Uniformed guards were employed, a system of badge identification of employees was instituted, and evidence of American citizenship, or government clearance in the case of the foreign-born, was required of all employees. This strict plant security program was maintained throughout the war, and owing to the company's continued participation in defense work has remained in effect ever since.

A prosperous year—December, 1941.

BY December, 1941, the management of Sangamo could look forward to the conclusion of an extremely prosperous year. The company was not only manufacturing commercial products at the fastest rate in its history, but in spite of disappointments and vicissitudes was establishing itself in the defense program. Eighteen thousand square feet of manufacturing space had been added by the construction of an addition to the building completed in 1939. Sales promised to reach a new high of $6,000,000 by the end of the year.

War —A challenge to American industry.

AND then came suddenly and stunningly the news! The Japs had attacked Pearl Harbor! In the days that followed came stark realization of what lay ahead. With the U. S. Pacific Fleet largely sunk or disabled, with vast quantities of shipping needed to fight a war on many fronts around the globe, with huge stores of military equipment of every sort urgently demanded to meet the omnivorous needs of the Army, the Navy and the Air Force, which would now expand as never before in history, there would be unprecedented demands upon American industry and upon the American worker. Sangamo, as well as almost every other American manufacturer, must gear for total war. For this conflict would not be won by men alone. This was a war in which industrial production and "know-how" would play a part equaling or perhaps surpassing that of manpower, a struggle in which the brains and manufacturing capacity of American industry would be a means to victory.

By providing the Allied military forces with more and superior equipment, American industry could save innumerable lives and hasten the day of victory. But to do this was no simple undertaking. The Axis powers were off to a formidable head-start and were producing at full thrust. Their war plans had been carefully matured over a long period of years and their whole economy was harnessed for war. Despite the acceleration of the last two years, the United States was far behind. It must catch up and go ahead, and it must do so quickly if at all.

PRODUCTION of non-essentials was curtailed at once. Strict governmental controls were imposed in order that each manufacturing unit might be fitted into the overall production scheme, that raw materials might be allocated where they were most seriously needed, and that skills and manufacturing knowledge might be pooled. Some of industry's top men took positions with government to help administer the program. While the controls

Industry gears for total war— 1942.

were often irksome, they were never applied to the point of stifling scientific or technological initiative. Working under a cloak of censorship, the armed services called upon industry to meet production goals that would have been thought fantastic in time of peace. Lacking confidence in industry at first, the procurement officers of the armed services eventually abandoned unnecessary "spit and polish," and brought their procurement policies into closer conformity with practical manufacturing procedures as manufacturers and workers demonstrated what they could do. Soon industry and the military services were working as a team. Technological advancement was phenomenal, especially in the field of electronics, where Sangamo was destined to make its own most significant contributions to the national war effort

First order for submarine attack teachers—December 6, 1941

JUST the day before Pearl Harbor Sangamo received its first order for antisubmarine attack teachers to be built according to the principles worked out by the company's own engineers in the weeks since the Navy first broached the project. This apparatus enabled a submarine detecting crew to be trained on shore, so that by the time the men were assigned to a ship they knew how to handle the detecting apparatus and to maneuver into position to attack a submarine. Without the teacher, they would have been obliged to learn on shipboard, through long hours of practice and with all the expense and tie-up of desperately needed vessels involved in taking a surface ship as well as one or more submarines to sea for practice maneuvers.

Sangamo delivered its first attack teachers to the Navy in May, 1942. Their test performance was wholly satisfactory and the Navy put them into use at once. They were the first product involving complicated electronics ever to be manufactured by Sangamo. The company was justly proud of them, and especially of its contribution to their design. Many more of these teachers were manufactured throughout the war, and as a result of their success the Navy turned again and again to Sangamo for help in developing and manufacturing other electronic devices.

SIX days after Pearl Harbor, Sangamo was requested to make a self-synchronous motor or synchro as manufactured by the Kollsman Instrument Division of the Square D Company. Subsequent discussions with Kollsman revealed the practicability of Sangamo's producing a type of extremely sensitive aircraft tachometer, an instrument for measuring the revolutions per minute of an aircraft engine which enabled a pilot to regulate and synchronize engine speeds. Kollsman, as well as every other supplier of aircraft indicating instruments, was overwhelmed with orders as the expanded aircraft industry bent every effort to meet President Roosevelt's call for the production of 85,000 warplanes a year. Consequently, as a result of its connection with Kollsman, Sangamo now

Subcontractor for manufacture of Kollsman instruments— 1942–1947

undertook the manufacture of other Kollsman products until eventually the plant was turning out ˥a multiplicity of special aircraft electrical units, among them motors to drive radio compass tuning loops, transmitter and receiver radio compass indicators, and a complete electrical instrumentation for Link trainers. This work ran into large volume throughout the war, and Sangamo continued to manufacture products for Kollsman until the end of January, 1947.

Total pro-
duction for war. WITHIN three weeks after Pearl Harbor Sangamo made its first cut in watthour meter production and by September 23, 1942, it had ceased producing commercial items altogether. The change-over to total war production was effected so efficiently that no employee lost a single day's work, and as Sangamo swung into line behind the national war effort employment rose from 1,550 in January to 2,075 in October. The purchase of the old Watch Factory buildings now proved itself to have been a most fortunate move; for with the increase in production and employment Sangamo was in pressing need of manufacturing space. Tenants in the old buildings were requested to find other accommodations, the whole plant was reconditioned, and the facilities for the assembly of war products were located in the Watch Factory buildings.

Expansion of
capacitor
operations—
1941-1943. SINCE the beginning of the war, Sangamo had experienced a steadily increasing demand for capacitors, inasmuch as this device is a component

used in a wide variety of electrical circuits. In its simplest form, it consists of two conductors separated by an insulating medium such as mica or paper, ranging from this through types requiring exacting manufacturing procedures. Sangamo had been manufacturing mica capacitors for almost eighteen years, although heretofore they had been a relatively unimportant item in the company's total output. As early as 1941, however, in response to requests from large users of this device, Sangamo began tooling for increased production. Since then, with the urgent need for all types of electronic equipment, the capacitor business had tremendously accelerated, until now, foreseeing an even greater demand from the armed services, Sangamo proposed to the War Production Board that facilities be immediately expanded. Nothing came of this proposal in Washington; but the Chicago Signal Corps Procurement Office, aware of the urgency, approved the necessary priorities for Sangamo to install equipment for a fourfold increase in production, and in March, 1942, the company undertook the expansion with its own capital.

Within five months the enormous demand for mica capacitors induced the Signal Corps and the War Production Board to sponsor a Defense Plant Corporation facilities contract with Sangamo, providing a further expansion of capacitor production. Within a little more than a year, not only was the production of mica capacitors fifty times what it had been two years before, with dollar volume greater than the entire sales of the company prior to 1941, but, at the request of the War Production Board, in 1943 the company began the manufacture of paper capacitors, a line which was continued in production through the balance of the war and further developed in the postwar period.

Subcontractor for Weston— summer, 1942.

THE demand for electrical indicating instruments such as ammeters and voltmeters was still increasing, and there was also some concern that east coast manufacturing installations might be bombed. Accordingly, the Weston Electrical Instrument Corporation was requested to expand its facilities somewhere west of the Allegheny Mountains. By reason of the close relations subsisting between Sangamo and Weston for many years, Weston proposed that Sangamo act as a subcontractor for the manufacture of some of its products so that Weston might concentrate upon the manufacture of certain devices that it alone was qualified to make. Consequently, in the summer of 1942, a facilities contract, sponsored by the Navy, was negotiated in the amount of $330,000 to provide Sangamo with special purpose tools and equipment. The arrangement contemplated the production of some 35,000 instruments per month, and from the beginning of production in June, 1943, until the termination of the arrangement in December, 1944, Sangamo turned out almost 400,000 of these instruments.

EVEN with government sponsorship and aid, tools and dies were difficult to obtain, so, in order to have a controlled supply of these essentials, Sangamo purchased the Allied Tool and Machine Company, a Chicago corporation employing skilled tool and die makers. Within a year the big job of tooling was accomplished, and with an assured supply of further requirements from its own plant and other sources, Sangamo resold the Allied company to its former owners.

Purchase of Allied Tool and Machine Company— August, 1942.

BY this time, the draft and the insatiable manpower demands of industry were creating or threatening labor shortages in many areas. In September, 1942, Sangamo's directors rescinded their ruling with respect to compulsory retirement of employees at age 65, inasmuch as many of the workers who would have been affected possessed irreplaceable skills, and all could be used to advantage in the stepped-up production program. As a matter of fact, while Sangamo faced serious employment problems, it experienced less trouble than did many other companies because it had always employed a high percentage of women on light machine work and assembly. Many manufacturers were plagued by absenteeism, but this was never very critical at Sangamo. There was some increase, to be sure, but it was due mainly to the fact that people were working long hours and must take time off for their normal personal affairs. When the banks and stores began keeping open on certain nights each week, the situ-

Loyalty and skill of Sangamo workers.

ation was eased at Sangamo as it was all over the country. The company posted monthly reports of absenteeism, male and female, by departments, with three percent marked as the danger line. Employees responded loyally, without the rewards some companies found it necessary to offer, and absences seldom reached the danger point.

Need for more working capital —August, 1942. THE volume of war business became so great that an increase in working capital became imperative, and the directors authorized borrowings not to exceed $2,000,000 under Regulation "V" of the Federal Reserve System. Later the authorization was increased to $4,000,000, a sum that would have seemed staggering a few years before; but no more than $2,000,000 was ever drawn.

Manufacture of many novel products—1943 BY the beginning of 1943, Sangamo was working three shifts around the clock, and was manufacturing and developing products with which it was entirely unfamiliar just a few months before—portable anemometers to indicate wind speed and direction for the Signal Corps, extremely sensitive relays for use in mines and depth charges and a special timing mechanism for Navy Ordnance, a variety of electrical indicating instruments of one sort or another. It was an undertaking calling for the best in engineering and manufacturing technique, for all the instruments must be precise, and some of them must be shock proof and impervious to quick changes in temperature, air pressure and humidity.

SO critical was the need for war materials of all sorts and so novel were some manufacturing procedures, that neither the government nor the prospective manufacturer could estimate costs with any degree of accuracy. Consequently, the government was protected by a stipulation of the National Defense Appropriation Act that provided for examination of the manufacturer's records, with renegotiation of contracts and recapture of profits in cases where they proved to be excessive. Like other companies, Sangamo was subject to these provisions. Even after renegotiation, however, sales for 1943 reached a new high of over $11,000,000. Employment was at a wartime peak of 3,080. Three hundred and fifty Sangamo employees were now in the armed services, 45 of whom were women.

Renegotiation of contracts— 1943. A year of tremendous production.

AT the annual meeting of the stockholders in 1943, Sangamo increased the number of its directors from nine to eleven. Mrs. Jacob Bunn and Mrs. Robert C. Lanphier, who had served faithfully since replacing their husbands as directors, resigned. Walter Robbins and Robert E. Miller also retired from the board after many years of useful service. The following were elected as the new board: Herbert B. Bartholf, George W. Bunn, Jr., Jacob Bunn, Jr., Willard Bunn, Donald S. Funk, J. Henry Hodde, Frederick C. Holtz, Charles H. Lanphier, Robert C. Lanphier, Jr., Herbert I. Markham and Carl A. Sorling.

Increase in number of directors— April, 1943.

Manufacture of meters resumed —1944.   The gigantic expansion of manufacturing facilities, the construction of military camps and immense defense housing projects, added to all the other unusual demands imposed by war, brought tremendous increases in consumption of electric power. This power must be measured and conserved; and near the end of 1943 the War Production Board authorized production of 150,000 singlephase, watthour meters during the next six months. Sangamo's allotment, as one of four manufacturers, was 40,000. As a result of this authorization the company resumed the manufacture of meters, although it did so without interference with its war work.

Sangamo designs new submarine detecting apparatus—1944–1945.   AS American scientists and technicians sought to develop ever more effective instruments of war, one of the National Research Laboratories devised a new system of submarine detection; and the Navy chose Sangamo to perfect the practical application of the idea. This was the first submarine detecting apparatus designed and manufactured entirely by Sangamo. In the spring of 1945 the first unit was installed in a destroyer for deep-sea tests off the Atlantic coast. Other destroyers were standing by, and in the course of the tests one of them picked up a radio message reporting that a freighter had just been torpedoed by a submarine not very far off. The whole flotilla steamed away in pursuit, and as the ships approached the designated spot the destroyer carrying Sangamo's new equipment picked up the U-boat. The raider was sunk. And inasmuch as the incident occurred on the Saturday night before V-E Day, the marauder may well have been the last U-boat to be destroyed.

An amusing incident occurred in connection with another test of submarine detecting equipment in which Charles H. Lanphier participated as a representative of the company. A destroyer and a submarine were to work together in the tests, and as the commanders of the respective vessels discussed procedures before leaving base, the sub commander asked the destroyer captain how deep he should submerge. The captain suggested 150 feet. But the Army-Navy football game was being played that afternoon and the submarine's radio antenna, attached to the periscope, submerged at 55 feet. The skipper was reluctant to go below that level, since to do so would cut off the football broadcast, so the tests were run off at 55 feet until, late in the afternoon when Army had piled up a commanding lead, the disconsolate submarine commander signalled that he would go down to 200 feet, or even to the bottom, if the captain gave the word.

AS Sangamo developed more intricate apparatus for the armed services, especially for the Navy, company engineers were sent to various military training centers to supervise tests or to instruct the service personnel in the use of the new equipment. The Navy also established a training school at the plant, where the men who were to service and repair the various instruments not only attended classes but

Training military technicians.

also studied every manufacturing process as the apparatus passed along the assembly lines. From twelve to eighteen of these trainees, under the command of a petty officer, were in the plant most of the time, and as the equipment was completed and shipped, these technicians—radio men, mechanics, electricians—were sent to Iceland, North Africa, England, Australia, the Pacific islands, as the case might be, right along with the equipment they were to maintain The company not only provided plant men to conduct these training courses, but in some cases even found lodgings for the trainees The Navy required the men to drill for at least an hour a day, so the petty officer would take them across the street from the plant and put them through exercises and maneuvers, matters on which he confessed he must do some brushing up himself.

Burdens imposed by government contracts. ARMY and Navy inspectors in varying numbers were in the plant throughout the war to check on the quality of the product at every stage of manufacture. Bookkeeping methods must be brought into accord with government accounting practice; and since the company was held strictly responsible for every item of allocated material, it had to work out systems to keep track of them at every stage. Altogether, there was a prodigious increase in paper work.

NOTWITHSTANDING the tremendous increase in volume of business resulting from the war, Sangamo's profits actually declined due to renegotiation and excess profits taxes. During the war years—1942 through 1945—sales after renegotiation averaged $11,053,085 per year as against $4,837,861 in the four preceding years of peace Yet profits for the war years averaged only $558,887 as against an average of $595,748 in the four preceding years. Thus the percentage of dollar volume retained by the company as profit not only declined from an average of 12.31 percent to 5.06 percent, but profits also showed an actual dollar decrease averaging $36,861 per year.

Comparison of profits in peace and war.

AT the beginning of 1944, Sangamo was obliged to modify its Pension Plan, with its 50-50 contributions from employer and employee, in order to conform with certain Treasury Department rulings. Under the plan as revised, Sangamo assumed the payment of all costs instead of requiring a contribution from employees as heretofore. To provide a more adequate retirement income, the company instituted the Retirement Income Plan, which provided for a supplemental retirement wage. Thus, at retirement, an employee of fifteen years service now receives an annual income equivalent to 35 percent of his last annual wage, his income increasing to 40 percent for thirty or more years of service.

The Retirement Income Plan— January 1, 1944

*A labor election
—December,
1944.*

SINCE 1937, eligible employees had bargained with the Sangamo management through the Selco Employees Association, an independent union. In December, 1944, as a result of an election conducted by the National Labor Relations Board, employees selected the Selco Employees Association to represent the production and maintenance workers, the International Association of Machinists to represent the tool and die makers, and the American Federation of Labor to represent the steam plant employees. These unions have continued to represent their respective units, and relations between management and employees have remained harmonious.

*Discontinuance
of the Weston
subcontracting
agreement
Production in
1945*

ON December 31, 1944, Sangamo closed out its subcontracting agreement with the Weston Electrical Instrument Corporation under which the Springfield company had manufactured a variety of instruments of Weston design. That company, together with other regular instrument manufacturers, could now handle the whole volume of government business and Sangamo, having helped meet the emergency, was left free to produce and develop other military apparatus. During the following year the War Production Board substantially increased the number of standard watthour meters to be manufactured to meet the requirements of the public utility companies, and by the end of the year Sangamo was making about half as many meters as would have constituted its normal pre-war output. These meters were not classed as civilian goods, but were channelled through the Office of War Utilities. Added to Sangamo's other war work, they taxed the company's productive facilities and manpower to the limit. Again sales established a new record, $13,500,000 after renegotiation.

IN the summer of 1945, Sangamo was tooling for the manufacture of additional war products. On August 14, however, came V-J Day, and hostilities ceased. At that time Sangamo was manufacturing military apparatus at its maximum rate. *Cessation of hostilities*

AS early as December 5, 1942, Sangamo had been awarded the Army-Navy "E" in recognition of its contribution to the war effort. The following June it was awarded its first star, which was followed by three similar awards at six months' intervals Thus Sangamo was one of a few companies to receive five citations for excellence; and in addition it was cited for excellence in plant security, and by the Navy's Bureau of Ships and Bureau of Ordnance for extraordinary engineering and manufacturing contributions. Sangamo Weston received the British Empire Medal for its war service, the award being made by King George VI in person. At the conclusion of hostilities the armed services had claimed 490 of Sangamo's employees, 60 of them women. Twelve gold stars were conspicuous on the company's service flag, and the names of those who died were inscribed on a memorial erected on the company grounds in 1948. *Citations for excellence.— Employees' service record— 1942–1945.*

Problems of reconversion— 1945

NOW, with the war ended, came immediate cancellation of military orders and the problems of reconversion to a peacetime basis of operations. The company was fortunate in having been permitted to resume production of meters during the last two years, for this business could now be continued and expanded while other production facilities were changing over for manufacture of normal lines. There was a heavy backlog of meter business and demand for capacitors far exceeded what it had been before the war. Time switches and tachographs were also in demand and some Navy contracts were continued. Major problems confronting the company were the procurement of raw materials, many of which were in short supply by reason of nation-wide strikes, and price ceilings, which were too often maintained rigidly despite increased costs due to wage and raw material price increases.

Adjustment to peacetime production—1946.

BECAUSE of these and other reconversion difficulties the company was obliged, soon after V-J Day, to lay off about 500 of its 2,664 employees. Many of these, however, were women who had been working only as a war measure; and before long employment was again on the increase. Some price relief was granted on capacitors almost immediately, and further adjustments came throughout the year. Even so, Sangamo, like industry in general, was in almost constant negotiation with the Office of Price Administration as government tried to combat inflation and industry sought relief from controls under which it was difficult if not impossible to operate.

AS the employment situation eased, Sangamo re- *Changes in execu-* instituted compulsory retirement at age 65. *tive personnel—* Under this rule, J. H. Hodde resigned as secretary *1946.* after more than forty years of loyal service. Mr. Hodde continued as a director of the company for two more years when he was succeeded on the board by Russell C. Bennett. Two other executive vacancies were occasioned in 1946 by the death of Charles R. Horrell, vice-president and sales manager, who had been with the company for 27 years, and the retirement of Charles Goin Lanphier, another vice-president with a long and active record. These losses necessitated reorganization of the company's executive personnel, and Charles H. Lanphier was elected a vice-president, while Cecil L. Clark became secretary-treasurer.

AS the company entered upon its first full year of *Plant additions* peacetime operations the chief problem was *at Springfield—* production rather than sales, and it soon became *1946.* apparent that additional manufacturing space would be needed to meet the pent-up demand for commercial products that had been in short supply for four years. Demand for singlephase watthour meters, for example, mounted steadily, with sales eventually reaching two and one-half times the highest pre-war figure. Polyphase meters, demand meters and thermal meters could be sold as fast as they could be made, and demand for capacitors had been tremendously increased by wartime developments.

To meet the need for additional space, it was decided to connect the Sangamo buildings with the Watch Factory structures in such a manner as to link the whole layout together as an efficient manufacturing unit. To do this, two new buildings were constructed, one designed to house the painting and plating department, and the other for the shipping department. Altogether, 30,000 square feet of manufacturing space were added with concomitant promotion of efficiency. A new Quonset warehouse provided an additional 10,000 square feet of storage space.

An increase in outstanding common stock— 1946

THE cost of the new buildings together with rehabilitation of the boiler room and necessary repairs to the Watch Factory buildings was in excess of $250,000, and was financed in large part by the sale of 8,000 shares of unissued common stock, thus making 286,000 shares of common stock outstanding.

The capacitor division moves to Marion— December, 1946.

EVEN with this increased capacity the company was pressed for space, and there were also forebodings of an impending labor shortage in Springfield. After a temporary dip, employment had now risen to 2,400. All returned veterans—some 300 to date—had been placed, and the company was experiencing increasing difficulty in filling its employment needs. Accordingly, the company officials made investigations of buildings immediately available in other cities and finally decided to lease space at the former Illinois Ordnance Plant from the War Assets Administration. Located in southern Illinois about equi-distant from Marion, Herrin and Carbondale, the proposed new plant was in an area well adapted to manufacturing enterprises and affording an ample labor supply. A five-year lease was signed, buildings were reconditioned and equipped, and by late December, 1946, the company's entire capacitor operations had been moved to the new location.

IN January, 1947, the company decided to expand its activities in the capacitor field still further by producing electrolytic capacitors. Engineers were employed to design the equipment and product and 50,000 additional square feet were rented from the government, bringing the total capacity of the Marion plant to 110,000 square feet. *Expansion at Marion—1947.*

THE year 1947 was the best in Sangamo's history up to that time, with sales, which had dropped to a postwar low of $9,904,000, now climbing back to a new record of $16,573,000. In Canada, Sangamo Limited, which was now operating in a modern, one-story factory in the northeast part of Toronto that had been completed during the war, was progressing so well that a new unit was purchased in the town of Newmarket, thirty miles north of Toronto, for the manufacture of mica and paper capacitors, radiosondes and certain other products which supplemented the output of the main factory. *Sales turn upward.—New plant facilities in Canada—1947.*

Postwar position of Sangamo Weston.

SANGAMO WESTON, which, besides experiencing labor and raw material problems, was confronted with the threat of nationalization of the British utility industry, had overcome the difficulties of reconversion and would soon be turning out meters, time switches and other instruments in excess of its pre-war rate. The British government, in accordance with its program of encouraging exports in order to supply itself with foreign exchange, was allocating materials to the company for volume production of meters for export to South Africa and South America.

Introduction of type H motor and S time switch, 1947–1948.

SANGAMO made substantial outlays for machinery, equipment and plant rearrangement in order to modernize thoroughly its Springfield plant. New commercial products were at a minimum in this period due to the complete preoccupation of the engineering staff through the war years with military designs The type H low speed hysteresis motor was introduced, and incorporated into the complete time switch line, singlephase and polyphase demand attachments, and the combination time switch watt-hour meter. Additionally, the new low-price small-size type S time switch was introduced to the market and a new type of instrument transformer with improved impulse insulation was announced.

Sales soar to all-time high— 1948

WHILE introducing these new items in the commercial field, the company also received new contracts from the Navy for both development and manufacture of equipment which had been under experimental development by the company during the war. In 1948, sales from the Springfield plant soared to a new all-time record of $21,139,000, and the number of employees increased to 2,732 of whom 440 were members of the Fifteen Year Club. Capacitor sales, which had amounted to $123,968 in the last year before the war, were now $1,255,000.

Thus Sangamo enters upon its fiftieth year of corporate existence, housed in modern quarters equipped with up-to-date machinery. Its finances are sound. Its workers are well paid and well provided for under a liberal retirement plan. Proud of its history, grateful for the loyalty and efficiency of its technological staff and working personnel, ready to assume its full measure of responsibility in peace or war, Sangamo faces the challenge of the future.

PRINTED BY

R R DONNELLEY & SONS COMPANY

CHICAGO

AND CRAWFORDSVILLE, INDIANA

CPSIA information can be obtained at www.ICGtesting.com
Printed in the USA
LVOW03s1023180714

394971LV00005B/29/P